THE SECRET TO LOVE, HEALTH, AND MONEY

A MASTERCLASS

THE SECRET TO LOVE, HEALTH, AND MONEY

A MASTERCLASS

Rhonda Byrne

ATRIA PAPERBACK

New York   London   Toronto   Sydney   New Delhi

ATRIA
PAPERBACK

An Imprint of Simon & Schuster, Inc.
1230 Avenue of the Americas
New York, NY 10020

Creative direction and artwork by Nic George

Graphic art and design by Josh Hedlund and Graphic design and artwork by
Josh Hedlund for Making Good, LLC.

Titles were previously published separately in audio format by
Simon & Schuster Audio in 2020.

This Atria Paperback edition February 2022

ATRIA PAPERBACK and colophon are trademarks of Simon & Schuster, Inc.

For information about special discounts for bulk purchases,
please contact Simon & Schuster Special Sales at 1-866-506-1949 or
business@simonandschuster.com.

The Simon & Schuster Speakers Bureau can bring authors to your live event.
For more information or to book an event, contact the Simon & Schuster Speakers
Bureau at 1-866-248-3049 or visit our website at www.simonspeakers.com.

Manufactured in the United States of America

3 5 7 9 10 8 6 4

ISBN 978-1-9821-8860-3
ISBN 978-1-9821-8861-0 (ebook)

Dedicated to you.

May The Secret bring you love and joy for your entire existence.

That is my intention for you, and for the world.

CONTENTS

THE SECRET TO HEALTH

THE SECRET TO MONEY

THE SECRET TO LOVE

Introduction
The Secret to Love

Fourteen years ago my life collapsed around me. I'd worked myself into exhaustion, I was grief-stricken over the sudden death of my father, and my relationships with my work colleagues and loved ones were in absolute turmoil. It was then that I discovered a secret that changed every aspect of my life, including my health, finances, and my relationships. I then decided to share this knowledge with the world—and since that time The Secret has helped tens of millions of people's lives worldwide. It can most definitely help your life too, and your relationships.

If you have attracted this book into your life, then perhaps you want to improve or heal the relationships in your life, or maybe attract new ones. You might be looking for your perfect partner, or want to restore a marriage, improve your relationships with your work colleagues, restore relationships with family or friends, or find new friends. The Secret that I discovered can help you achieve all of this, and much, much more.

With The Secret you can be, do, or have anything you want, in every area of your life.

But when you think about it, it's the relationships that give true meaning to your life. Without someone to share it with, there's probably very little that you would truly want to be, do, or have.

Imagine if you were the only person on Earth; you would have no desire to be, do, or have anything. What would be the point in creating a painting if no one could see it? What would be the point in composing music if no one could hear it? What would be the point in inventing anything if there was no one to use it? There would be no reason to move from one place to another, because wherever you went would be the same as where you were—no one would be there. There would be no pleasure or joy in your life. *It's your contact and experiences with other people that give your life joy, meaning, and purpose.*

Your relationships provide you with great opportunities to transform your life through positive thoughts and feelings. That's because the more gratitude we feel for our relationships, and the more kindness we show others, the more our entire life improves. And equally, the more love you have for the people in your life, the more love comes back to you, and the more amazing your entire life will be! Whatever you give—love, gratitude, kindness—comes back to you.

Your relationships affect your life in more ways than you can possibly imagine, so it makes sense that happy, loving relationships should be a priority for us all. This book will show you exactly how to create great relationships. You will see first-hand the transformation that can happen across all areas of your life—your finances, health, personal goals and dreams—and in your joy and happiness.

Lesson 1

Love and the Law of Attraction

The entire universe is governed by natural laws. We can fly in an airplane because aviation works in harmony with natural laws. The laws of physics didn't change for us to be able to fly, but we found a way to work in accordance with the natural laws so we can fly. Just as laws of physics govern aviation, electricity, and gravity, there is a law that governs our life. To improve or restore a relationship, or attract a new one, you must understand this law, the most powerful law in the universe—the law of attraction.

From the greatest to the smallest—the law of attraction is what holds every star in the universe and forms every atom and molecule. The attraction of the sun holds the planets in our solar system, keeping them from hurtling into space. Attraction in gravity holds you and every person, animal, plant, and mineral on Earth. Attraction can be seen in all of nature, from a flower attracting bees or a seed attracting nutrients from the soil, to every living creature being attracted to its own species. Attraction operates through all the animals on the Earth, fish in the sea, and birds in the sky, leading them to multiply and form herds, schools, and flocks. Attraction holds together the cells of your body, the materials of your house, and the furniture you sit on. It holds your car to the road and the water in your glass. In fact, every object you use is held together by the force of attraction.

Attraction is also the force that draws people to other people. It draws people to form groups, communities, and societies where they share common interests. It is the force that pulls one person to science and another to the arts. It pulls people to various sports, and to different styles of music and fashion, and to certain animals and pets. Attraction is the force that draws you to your favorite things and places, and it's the force that draws you to your friends and the people you love.

The law of attraction is the all-powerful law that keeps everything in harmony, from atoms to countless galaxies. It is operating in everything and through everything, all across the universe. And it is the law that is operating in your life.

How exactly does it work in your life? *Quantum physics* explains that everything in the Universe is made of energy vibrating at a certain frequency, and that includes your thoughts. Thoughts are also made of energy; they can be measured, and they each have a particular frequency. Your thoughts attract back to them people, circumstances, and events that are on the same frequency. Like attracts like, and through the law of attraction the things you think about the most are what come into your life. In other words, you create your life through your thoughts. Everything that comes into your life you have attracted into your life through the thoughts you've been thinking.

Like all the laws of nature, the law of attraction is immutable; no one is above it or excluded from it. It is impersonal, and operates on all of us equally—on every subject, and on every single thought.

Relationships and the Law of Attraction

What the law of attraction means in simple terms for your relationships is: whatever you *think* about your relationships is what you will *attract* into your relationships. You can't have thoughts of dissatisfaction about a relationship and then enjoy a relationship filled with love. For example, you can't think, "They don't love me as much anymore," and have the experience of that person loving you even more. You have to think thoughts of love to attract back love in return. You are a magnet in this Universe, and whatever you think, by the law of attraction, will return to you in your life through people, circumstances, and events.

It's like the old adage: whatever you sow, you reap! The thoughts that you think are the seeds, and the harvest you reap will depend on the type of seeds you plant. Think positive thoughts and you will attract positive people, circumstances, and events into your life. Think negative thoughts and you will be surrounded by negative people, circumstances, and events. It is the physics of the mind and the mathematics of the universe. Because as more physicists are discovering—this is a mental Universe.

So let's define positive thoughts and negative thoughts.

Positive thoughts are thoughts of what you want! Negative thoughts are thoughts of what you don't want.

In any moment you're thinking, you're either thinking positive thoughts or negative thoughts. And whether they're positive or negative will determine what you attract back into your relationships and your life. All the people, circumstances, and events that make up every single moment of your life are being attracted back to you through the thoughts you're thinking. What you are living now is because of what you have thought before. When you don't know how powerful your thoughts are in creating your life, you can see how easy it is to bring the very things you don't want into your life. But that will change from now with what you are discovering.

If you are thinking positive thoughts, then you attract positive people, positive circumstances, and positive events. But if you are thinking negative thoughts, or angry thoughts, then you can expect negative and angry people, circumstances, and events to come into your life.

Life doesn't just happen to you, and the state of your relationships is not random; you have attracted everything in your life based on what you've thought. Think positively about other people, and all that positivity will most surely come back to you in your relationships and lift up every other area of your life.

Think negatively about others through thoughts of complaining, blaming, anger, or any other negative ideas, and you will attract that negativity back into your life—guaranteed! And as the negativity comes back, it causes more negative thoughts, attracting more negativity, and on and on it goes.

The same thing happens if you're listening to someone else complain and you focus on their complaint. As you sympathize with them and agree with them, in that moment you are attracting more situations and people to blame and complain about. This is true no matter how valid the complaints or reasons to blame others.

One woman I heard from was going through a very unhappy period in her romantic life. Counselors traced the reasons all the way back to abusive relationships she experienced in her childhood. However, the woman came to see that her tendency to complain and blame others for the problems in her life was also contributing to her bad relationships. It was only when she stopped looking for reasons to complain and blame others, and instead looked for reasons to love and to appreciate the people in her life, that things began to change.

Almost immediately after this change in her thinking, she was introduced to her perfect partner. From his personality and values all the way to his eye color and hair, he was the man of her dreams. Within three months they were engaged, and two years later, they married. The remarkable thing about this couple is that their lives had coincidentally intertwined over the course of twenty years. They unknowingly shared family connections, holiday destinations, and they even worked in the same company for three years . . . yet they had never met. It was almost as if the Universe kept them apart until the fateful day that this woman realized the need to stop complaining and blaming others. In truth, that's exactly what happened.

The Blame Game

Words are very powerful; by the law of attraction, whatever you think or say about another person, you bring to you. When you blame or complain about any person, you actually harm *your* life. It is *your* life that will suffer.

Blaming and complaining are powerful forms of negativity. They bring so much strife. With every little complaint and every moment you blame someone else, you are attracting back to yourself a whole lot of situations going wrong that will cause you to complain. Complaints about the government, your partner, children, parents, neighbors, long lines, the economy, food, work, customers, businesses, prices, noise, or service seem like small, harmless things. But they bring back with them a whole host of negativity, which will affect your relationships and your whole life.

If you get annoyed because there was a mix-up in an appointment, and you blame the other person for the mix-up, you are using blame as your excuse not to think positively. But the law of attraction only responds to what *you're* thinking, regardless of the situation, so if you're blaming, you must receive circumstances of blame back in your life. They won't necessarily come back to you from the person you were blaming, but most assuredly you will receive circumstances of blame. There are no excuses for the law of attraction. Whatever your dominant thoughts are is what you will receive back in your life. You are creating your future life with the thoughts you are thinking right now!

It's also true that the more you think about the things you love, the more things you will receive back that you love. When you think thoughts of what you love, no matter who or what those thoughts are about, that love returns to you, bringing circumstances that you love. As you love the new circumstances that have appeared, that then attracts more positive things, adding even *more* love and positivity to your life, and so it continues. Therefore, to attract more love into your life, all you have to do is think thoughts of what you love.

I know of one couple in particular where this led to the most amazing turnaround in their marriage. They had only been married a short time when the relationship was beginning to stagnate. They were virtually living separate lives. Even though she could barely stand to sleep in the same bed as her husband, the wife was determined to save her marriage. What she did was to note all of the small things that

*he did for her, and to let him know how much
she appreciated him. Suddenly, he could not do
enough for her. They began to laugh and play
together once more, and the passion returned.*

There is a saying, most often attributed to Gandhi,
that goes like this: "You must *be* the change you
wish to *see* in the world."

What this young wife did was to apply that same
notion to her marriage. If you wish to change
a relationship in your life, then you have to be
the change by changing how you think about
the relationship. The more positive thoughts
of love, appreciation, and gratitude you have
for your relationship, the more you will attract
back positive circumstances and events in your
relationship. You have to *be* the change you want
to *see* in your relationship! And all you have to
do is change your thoughts. Doing that one thing
changes everything!

Ask yourself: Are you thinking enough positive
thoughts in your relationships? Because positive
thoughts come from and are based in love,
whereas negative thoughts are the absence of love.

You can tell in your relationships right now how
many positive thoughts you've been thinking. If a
current relationship is great, it means you've been

thinking more positive thoughts than negative thoughts. If a current relationship is difficult or challenging, it means you are inadvertently thinking more negative thoughts about the relationship than positive.

Always remember: as challenging as it might be to hear, it's not about the other person. Some people think a relationship is either good or bad because of the other person, but life doesn't happen that way. You can't say to the law of attraction, "I will think positive thoughts only when the other person changes!" You can't receive anything in life unless you give it first! Whatever you give, you receive, so it's not about the other person at all: it's all about you! It's all about what you are thinking, what you are emitting, what you are giving. Because when you think positive thoughts about others, you will have amazing relationships, and you will have an amazing life.

LESSON 2

THE POWER OF THOUGHTS AND FEELINGS

You can change your life and you can change your relationships, because you have an unlimited ability to think positive thoughts. When you think about what you want and what you love, you bring everything good in life to you, including good people and good relationships!

According to the law of attraction, what you think is the primary cause of everything in your life. That includes your health, your job, your financial situation, your living conditions, and all of your relationships. Whatever you think about you bring about, which means that everything you see and experience in this world is *effect*. The *cause* is always your thoughts.

Feelings: Rocket Fuel for Your Thoughts

If you're concerned that a random thought that pops into your head could change the course of your life, you can relax. You think so many thoughts in a day that don't amount to anything because many of your thoughts don't elicit a strong feeling within you. Your thoughts are amplified when strong feelings are added to them. And you always have strong feelings when you believe your thoughts to be true!

Let me explain it this way: imagine your thoughts as a rocket ship, and your feelings as the fuel. A rocket ship is a stationary vehicle that can't do anything without fuel, because the fuel is the power that lifts the rocket ship. It's the same with your thoughts. Without your feelings, your thoughts don't have the same power. While your thoughts remain the primary cause of everything, your feelings are the accelerant to make your thoughts manifest faster. The stronger you feel about something you are thinking about, the more power you are adding to that thought, and the sooner that thought manifests in your life.

Your feelings also serve another purpose: they help you to know what kind of thoughts you're thinking. Good thoughts always cause good feelings, whereas bad thoughts cause bad feelings. So if you want to know whether you're thinking positive or negative thoughts, just be aware of how you're feeling. Whenever you're feeling good, you can be certain that the thoughts you've been thinking have also been good. Whenever you don't feel good, it's a sign that you've been thinking negative thoughts, and you will want to pay more attention to what you're thinking.

How you feel about any given relationship is also caused by your thoughts about that relationship. If you feel happy or grateful about a relationship, for example, then you know you've been thinking positive thoughts about it. If you feel angry or frustrated about a relationship, then you know you've been thinking negative thoughts about it.

If you think, "I can't stand my boss," there's likely a strong negative feeling that comes with that thought, and by the law of attraction, you will attract situations where your relationship with your boss continues to get worse.

If you think, "I work with some fabulous people in my job," there's likely a strong positive feeling that comes with that thought, and you will attract situations where your relationships with your work colleagues continue to get even better.

Or to put it in simple terms:

The more good thoughts you think, the better you feel and the better life gets.

The more bad thoughts you think, the worse you feel and the worse life gets—until you change how you're thinking.

> *One woman had been at the same job for ten years and was very unhappy, not so much with the work she did, but more with the people she worked with. The problem was that she was surrounded by gossip, constant complaining, and negativity. And without realizing it, she had been drawn in to behave the same way. Like her colleagues, she found that she never had anything nice to say. Once she became aware of her part in all this, she made a conscious effort to be happy and enthusiastic in her work, and to avoid all gossip. The response was virtually instantaneous. Within days, she began to enjoy her work. And by refusing to feed into the negativity, she found that the gossipers and complainers no longer shared*

*their gripes with her. She made no effort to avoid
them. She simply elected to see the best in them,
which meant that she saw less and less of them.
Meanwhile, she found herself surrounded by a
new set of work friends who were fun and positive
and enjoyed spending time together. Better still,
one of these new work friends went on to become
her boyfriend, and they have plans to marry.*

*Simply by thinking good thoughts and remaining
positive in her job, this woman not only attracted
better relationships, she transformed her whole
life!*

Change Any Relationship

When you change the way you think about a
relationship, you change the thoughts you are
emitting, and the relationship *must* change to
mirror your new way of thinking. It's as simple as
that.

Even if you can't imagine how a particular
relationship can change into something positive,
know that it can!

If you are in a challenging relationship with
someone, there's a very simple and powerful

practice you can use that takes just a few minutes each day. Simply feel love within your heart for the other person, and then open your heart and send that love out into the Universe. Just doing this one thing helps to remove any resentment, anger, or negativity you might have within you toward that person.

On the other hand, you will never improve a relationship with negativity. Feeling resentment, anger, or any negative emotion toward another person attracts it back to you. When you are feeling love, it attracts love back to you. What you are feeling for another, you are bringing to you. If you find it difficult to feel good about a particular person or relationship, then focus on loving everything else around you. And do the very best you can to stop giving your attention to any of the negative things in the relationship.

You have the power to change anything, because you are the one who chooses your thoughts and you are the one who feels your feelings. This means you can change any negative relationship in your life, but you can't change it by remaining negative; you can't change it with negative thoughts and negative feelings. You have to react differently to the relationship, because if you keep reacting negatively, those thoughts will magnify and multiply any negativity. When you have good thoughts and good feelings, the good things in the relationship must magnify and multiply.

Two best friends fell out over something quite trivial, but when they didn't speak for months, it appeared as though their friendship had come to an end. One of the women was so upset, she felt as though she had fallen into an "unhappiness hole." Eventually she decided to change her life for the better, and so she committed to being positive and feeling happy. Despite a number of stressful things going on in her life, she managed to elevate herself to a point where she was feeling fulfilled. Around this time, a mutual friend asked her if she'd made up with her best friend. She answered no, they hadn't spoken, but she was sure that soon they would be friends once again. That night, she found herself in such a good mood that she felt compelled to make a list of all the blessings in her life. She went to bed feeling better than she had in a long time. The very next morning, she received a message from her best friend saying how much she missed their friendship and how sorry she was that they had fought.

For these two best friends, it was not until they were able to elevate their thoughts about one another that the law of attraction was able to reunite them.

The Power of Feeling Good

Whenever you are faced with a negative situation in a relationship, the solution is always to think good thoughts and feel good despite what is happening in the relationship. You won't know *how* it will be solved, but if you maintain your positive thoughts and feel good, it will happen. When you are feeling good, then only people who are on the same frequency as you are can come into your life.

Just be aware that feeling love toward people who you might be having a difficult time with doesn't mean you let them walk all over you or abuse you. That's certainly not love either. Allowing another person to use you doesn't help that person, and it surely doesn't help you. The answer is, get yourself onto the highest frequency of good feelings that you can, and the law of attraction will resolve the situation *for* you.

If you maintain your frequency of good feelings while someone in your life remains at a negative frequency, the law of attraction will keep you apart. A relationship ending between two people is the *result* of the two people no longer being on the same frequency. When the frequencies of people are no longer a match, the law of attraction automatically responds by moving them apart.

It can be quite fascinating to see the way the law of attraction reacts to the changing frequencies of people.

One young woman met a man straight out of high school who swept her up in a whirlwind romance. She left her hometown, her family, and her friends to follow him far away in search of work and a new life. They married a couple of months later. However, she soon discovered a dark side to her new husband in the form of substance abuse as well as some undiagnosed mental problems. Through his frequency of anger, he constantly lashed out at the first person he saw—his wife. He was verbally abusive, hurling the most demeaning insults her way. With no support network of family and friends, she was unable to cope or to think enough good thoughts to lift her own frequency. She fell into a deep depression. For five long years, she endured a loveless, abusive marriage, spending much of her time trying to avoid this angry man in her own home.

Eventually, she came to understand that only she could turn her life around and restore her own happiness. As if by coincidence, within weeks of receiving that insight, she and her husband decided to return to her hometown in search of work. As luck would have it, she found a great job straightaway, and she reconnected with friends and family. She was beginning to feel herself again for the first time in many years. But for her husband, things only got worse. He was unwilling to accept his wife's newfound success and happiness, and so he doubled down on the abuse. However, now that she was surrounded by support and love, and now that she was committed to happiness, his abuse could no longer affect her. As a consequence, their frequencies no longer matched, and the law of attraction responded by moving them apart. She finally left her husband as she came to realize that she was worthy of a far better life.

A short time later, she was invited out to dinner with friends. Afterward, they decided on a whim to stop in at a new bar in town. The moment she walked in the door, her eyes were drawn to the back of the room. There she saw the familiar face of a boy she had dated in high school; in fact, the last boyfriend she had before meeting her husband. A mutual friend pulled her aside and told her that this man had carried a torch for her all these years. Apparently, he had never had another serious girlfriend, as he'd been waiting for her all this time. Intrigued, she approached him and they reminisced awhile. He confirmed the story—that he had hoped and prayed she would come back home one day. He convinced himself that if she did, then it was a sign that they would be together forever. The longer they spoke, the more she came to realize that he was everything she had dreamed about in a partner, and a new romance blossomed. They are now together, deliriously happy, and they plan to marry.

For this woman, her ex-husband's abuse and anger caused her to think negatively about the situation she found herself in, and those negative thoughts not only made her feel bad but led her into depression. It was only when she was able to change her frequency through positive thoughts of love and happiness that she could break free from her ex-husband. Once she was feeling good again, then only people on the same frequency could come into her life. So it is no surprise that the law of attraction delivered love to this woman in the form of her original high school sweetheart.

The Power Is In You

It doesn't matter how difficult or damaged a relationship is. If you want to change it you can begin to do so by simply changing your thoughts and changing your frequency.

Everything that you've received in your life is a result of what you've been thinking and how you are feeling, and that goes for *all* of your relationships, past and present.

It also means that any difficult relationships that you might be experiencing were attracted by your own past thoughts and feelings.

Often when people first hear this part of The Secret, they recall past difficult or even abusive relationships. They find it incomprehensible that anyone could have attracted that situation. No one would deliberately attract a challenging or difficult relationship into their life, but if your wish is to repair or resolve a difficult relationship, it is helpful to understand that you attracted it for a reason. Most of the time we attract difficult situations to ourselves to wake ourselves up to the inherent power we hold.

You have a choice right now. Do you want to believe that it's just the luck of the draw and bad things can happen to you at any time? Do you want to believe that you have no control over your relationships or the way people treat you?

Or do you want to believe and *know* that your life experience is now in your hands? Do you want to know that only *good* people, *good* circumstances, and *good* relationships can come into your life, because of the way you think? You have a choice, and whatever you choose to think will become your life experience.

Understand that no one can come into your life and affect you negatively unless you are on the same frequency. When you change your thoughts and raise your frequency, it won't matter how difficult or negative someone is, they will not and cannot affect you! And if that results in a difficult relationship coming to an end, don't despair. Repeat to yourself, "All good is coming from this situation." And it will. Learn from each experience. You will find that after experiencing the breakup of a difficult relationship, in time your level of joy will be higher than it has ever been before. Every relationship in your life is there for a reason, teaching you something and taking your life forward.

So often when things change in our lives, we have such resistance to the change. But it is important to remember that when something big changes in our lives, it means something better is coming. There cannot be a vacuum in the Universe, and so as something moves out, something must come in and replace it. When change comes, relax, have total faith, and know that the change is *all good*.

So don't be afraid of change, especially in your relationships. Remember that every single thing that happens is ultimately for the good of each of us. It is not what happens, but what we do with the opportunity, and how we choose to look at it, that matters. The Universe has to move things out to allow the better and more wonderful things to appear. Realize this change is happening because a more magnificent relationship is coming to you! Something better is coming.

LESSON 3

THE SECRET TO AMAZING RELATIONSHIPS

When you think of yourself living a great life with amazing relationships, you are powerfully and consciously determining your life through the law of attraction. It's truly that easy. But if it's that easy, why doesn't everybody have a great life with amazing relationships?

The problem is that most people think and talk about what they *don't* want *more* than they think and talk about what they *do* want. In doing so, they are inadvertently depriving themselves of all the good things in life, including wonderfully fulfilling relationships.

People who have great relationships think and talk about what they want *more* than what they *don't* want! And people with difficult relationships think and talk about what they *don't* want more than they think and talk about what they *do* want. As they think and talk so much about what they don't want in their relationships, they wonder why problems in their relationships keep showing up over and over and over again. But they actually attracted those problems into their lives simply by thinking and talking about what they *don't* want.

The law of attraction doesn't compute "don't" or "not" or "no," or any other words of negation. As you speak words of negation, like "don't want," the law of attraction hears the opposite.

When you say, "I don't want to argue."

The law of attraction hears, *"I want more arguing."*

When you say, "Don't speak to me like that."

The law of attraction hears, *"I want you to speak to me like that and I want other people to speak to me like that."*

When you think, "I don't want to lose them."

The law of attraction hears, *"I want to lose them."*

When you think, "I don't want to be lonely."

The law of attraction takes that to mean *"I want to be lonely."*

The law of attraction is giving you what you are thinking about—period!

The wife of an active air force officer found this out the hard way. Five years into their marriage, her husband left on his fifth overseas deployment. The wife became resentful and angry, and filled with thoughts of loneliness and abandonment. A lifelong pessimist, she had become overwhelmed by thinking and believing thoughts of what she didn't want. A short time later, she received a message from her husband advising that he planned to file for divorce. She was devastated. After a couple of days in despair, she decided to make the effort to change her way of thinking. She began to focus on the positive, and when she spoke with him, she took care to use kind and constructive words. She knew that she could not expect him to change his mind, but she remained optimistic, thinking only good thoughts, and feeling love. A few weeks later, he reached out to her with an offer to work through their problems. Happily, their marriage was saved thanks to the two of them focusing their thoughts on what they really wanted.

Focus on the Relationship You Want

Whether you think about the relationship you want or the relationship you don't want, *that* is what you are thinking into existence. And that is what is going to show up over and over and over again. If you really want to change a relationship, or bring a new one to you, you have to think exclusively about what you want and what makes you feel good, in order to bring it into existence.

If you focus completely on the things you want, on the things you like, and on what makes you feel good, then you will have a really great life.

Life presents everything to you so that you can choose what you want, what you like, and what you appreciate the most. And part of the gift of life is that you are given all kinds of people so you can choose what you like and appreciate in those people and turn away from what you don't. You are not meant to manufacture appreciation for a person's qualities that you don't like, but simply to turn away without judging them or giving them any more attention.

Turning away from what you don't like in someone means you're relaxed about it, and you know life is giving you a choice. It doesn't mean that you argue with them to prove they're wrong, or that you criticize them, or that you want to change them because you think you're right. If you do any of these things, you are definitely not focused on what you want and what you appreciate. You can't receive anything in life unless you think it first, so you have to think about what you want and appreciate in order to receive it. To improve any relationship, focus on the things you like and appreciate about the other person and on the wonderful things about the relationship, rather than focusing on the things you don't like.

A young woman discovered the outcome of focusing too much on things she didn't like about her partner. She had been caught up in a stormy relationship with a man for about a year, during which they had broken up four times. She had a gut feeling that things were never quite right, yet she kept persisting with this man, having convinced herself that he was "the one." She held out hope that he would change, and act the way she expected him to act. In conversation with her best friend, she decided to monitor her partner's behavior. If she saw no signs of improvement, she made a commitment to herself to break up with

him permanently. The next day, the man texted
to say that he was breaking up with her. And the
reason he gave was that he didn't consider her
good enough for him. By criticizing, finding fault,
and trying to change her partner, this woman had
attracted criticism, fault-finding, and the end of
the relationship.

An astounding statistic has come out of research studies into relationships. What they found is that for every *one* criticism about another person, whether in thought or word, there must be *ten* positive thoughts for the relationship to flourish. Any fewer than ten positive thoughts for every one critical thought and the relationship will deteriorate. If the relationship is a marriage, it is much more likely to end in divorce.

No relationship is perfect, but if you can find ten positive thoughts for every criticism, then you are on your way to appreciating that person just the way they are. After all, don't you want everyone close to you to love you just the way you are?

As an experiment, try appreciating your *im*perfect relationships by thinking positive thoughts about people just as they are! If you find yourself criticizing or finding fault in someone, correct yourself by looking for ten positive attributes in that person. Whenever you appreciate a relationship, even if it's not perfect, you will see it miraculously get better. And even if all of your relationships are currently good, they will increase with more magnificence through this experiment.

The Secret to Romance

When it comes to romance, many people invest countless hours and money into matchmaking services and dating apps, trying to find their perfect partner. But the law of attraction is the only true matchmaking service, and all you need to do is think and talk about the relationship you want. Think and talk about every positive thing you want in a partner, then sit back, feel good, and surrender to the Universe. Allow the Universe to bring your perfect partner to you, and to move you to them.

From our smaller perspective we can't see everything, but from its total perspective the Universe can see everything and it knows the perfect match for a person.

People may say that they want to attract love and be joyously happy in a relationship, but then they get caught up in the details of *who*. They think that a particular person is the one and only answer to their perfect relationship. But the Universe can see way into the future, and it knows if a particular person will fulfill your dreams or become your nightmare. When you don't receive the love from a particular person, you might think the law of attraction is not working. But it is working. If your *greatest* desire is to attract love and be joyously happy, then listen to the Universe. It is saying, "Not him or not her, and please get out of the way, I am trying to deliver the perfect person to you."

Be very careful about getting caught up in the who, where, when, or how, because you could block your greatest desire from being delivered to you.

One young woman was absolutely certain that she had met the love of her life. The only problem was, he didn't seem to feel the same way. He was caring and affectionate, but that's as far as it went. Nevertheless, she became consumed with thoughts of all the romantic things he would say to her. She even wrote a journal about their imaginary love story as though it were really happening. Yet all this fantasizing seemed to do was drive him further into the "friend zone." Over months and years, he would drift in and out of her life. So she made a pact with herself that if he returned once more, it was a sign from the Universe that they were meant to be together.

Around this time she began a new job where she met a man, and the strangest thing happened. He was everything she had been journaling about. They fell deeply in love in what she describes as the most beautiful connection and the happiest, most joyful love of her life. She now appreciates that the Universe was reacting to who she really, deeply wanted, rather than who she thought she wanted. And the Universe responded by offering her the perfect person who could provide her with everything she was asking for.

Trust in life more. This is a friendly Universe, and everything is happening *for* you. When it comes to relationships, too often people try to defy the law of attraction. They try to use the law of attraction to force someone to fall in love with them. But it just doesn't work like that. You can't jump into someone else's body and think their thoughts for them, you can only think your own thoughts. You create your life through what you think, and everyone else creates their life through their thoughts. And you wouldn't want it any other way, otherwise someone else could override your life with their thoughts. You are 100 percent free to create your life the way you want it to be, and everyone else is free to create their life exactly as they want it.

Your Wish Is My Command

You may have heard the law of attraction compared to Genie from Aladdin's lamp. Your thoughts are exactly like making wishes, and with every thought, Genie responds with *"Your wish is my command!"*

Genie assumes that everything you think about, you want. That everything you talk about, you want. That everything you act upon is what you want. Genie never questions your commands. You ask for it, and Genie immediately begins to leverage the Universe, through people, circumstances, and events, to fulfill your wish.

But remember, Genie has certain rules that he can't break, as he explains to Aladdin: *"I can't make anybody fall in love with anybody else!"*

And that is true of the law of attraction. You are in a partnership with the law of attraction, and it is through your partnership that you are creating *your* life. Whether they know it or not, every other person is in a partnership with the law of attraction as well, and they are creating *their* own life. That means you cannot use the law of attraction against another person's free will. If any of us attempted to rob someone else of their freedom, we would not only fail, but we would attract having our own freedom taken from us.

Each one of us is the creator of our own life, and we cannot create in someone else's life unless the other person is consciously wanting that same thing.

The correct use of law of attraction is to think about a happy, harmonious, loving relationship, and then allow the Universe to deliver your perfect partner to you, whoever they may be.

In fact, many people have written to me asking how they can use the law of attraction to *win back* the love of their life. As you now know, we can never override other people's freedom to choose for themselves. That's why both partners would have to want the same thing in order for it to manifest.

Since *The Secret* was released, I have seen thousands and thousands of people attract their perfect partner, hundreds of marriages saved, and countless broken relationships transformed into magnificent ones. To change any relationship, you simply must change the way you think about it. When you change the way you think about a relationship, everything about it will change.

Of all the relationships I know that have been restored through conscious use of the law of attraction, one particular story stands out. This woman simply decided to shift her attention from the things she didn't love in her partner to the things she did love.

The couple had been dating for a while, yet it was still very exciting and new. At this time, the woman described her partner as kind, generous, and incredible. However, she began to notice some similarities to her father, traits that she was not so fond of. For starters, he was inclined to be messy, leaving dishes on the counter, just like her dad. He would forget to call when he'd said he would, just like her dad. And he would shy away from discussing personal topics, just like her dad. She accused him of not taking her seriously, of not texting her enough, of not caring, and not loving her enough. Inevitably, he broke up with her, and she was heartbroken. She came to realize what she had lost, and that he was indeed a caring and sweet man. She accepted that the breakup was all her own doing, as she had obsessed over a few trifling flaws in among hundreds of wonderful qualities. She wanted to win him back, but she also let go by making the decision that she was going to be happy whether he decided to return to her or not. She spent the time alone reflecting upon the good times they had spent together, and gave no thought to the breakup. Eventually, he reached out to her. They were able to put their minor grievances aside and the romance was rekindled. Two years down the track and their love is stronger than it has ever been.

The remarkable thing that this woman did was to make the decision to be happy no matter what her ex-partner decided. In this kind of situation, you must be prepared to let go, no matter how hard that might seem. The tighter you try to hold on to something that you are afraid of losing, the more you are pushing it away. Those thoughts of trying to hold on are filled with fear, and if you persist, what you fear the most will come upon you.

Fear nothing—just think about what you want. It feels so much better!

LESSON 4

THE CREATIVE PROCESS FOR RELATIONSHIPS

The law of attraction lets you have, be, or do *anything* you want. So when it comes to a particular relationship, what do you *really* want?

You are a creator, and there is an easy process to follow to create any relationship you want. The greatest mystics, sages, philosophers, and thinkers have shared this Creative Process throughout history. It is the best way I know to harness the power of the law of attraction. It is an easy guideline for you to create what you want in three simple steps. Whether you want to find your perfect partner, have more love, a new friendship, or change something you don't like about an existing relationship, the process is always the same.

The First Step is to Ask.

You get to choose the relationship you want, but you must get very clear about what you want. If you're not clear, then the law of attraction cannot bring you what you want. You will be sending out a mixed signal, and you can then only attract mixed results. For the first time in your life perhaps, work out what it is you *really* want with a particular relationship.

The Second Step is to Believe.

You must believe that in the moment of asking, you have *already* received the relationship you want. You must have complete and utter faith. You must believe that you already have what you've asked for. When you believe you have that perfect relationship right now, the law of attraction will powerfully move all circumstances, people, and events for you to receive it.

The Third and Final Step in the Creative Process is to Receive.

Ask once, believe you have received, and all you have to do to receive that perfect relationship is feel good. When you are feeling good, you are on the receiving frequency. You are on the frequency of all good things coming to you, and you will receive what you have asked for. You wouldn't ask for a relationship unless it was going to make you feel good in the receiving of it, would you? So get yourself on the feeling-good frequency, and you will receive everything you want, not just wonderful relationships.

Let's look at using the Creative Process specifically to attract a new romantic relationship.

Step 1: ASK

If you want to attract your perfect partner, then get clear on the kind of relationship you want to have. What do you want the relationship to be like? List all of the things you want in the relationship. Love, companionship, mutual interests, laughter, intimacy, and happiness are just a few possible things.

Describe your perfect partner. Sit down and write out on a piece of paper all the positive qualities of your dream partner. Be sure to write it all in the present tense. Try to avoid thinking about a specific person and instead think about your ideal type. What are their interests? What do they look like? How do they dress? How do they earn a living? What do they like to do in their spare time? What are their values? Are they close with their family? What is their belief system? Are they open-minded? Are they disciplined? Do they love music? Sports? Do they like to party or are they a homebody? What kind of food do they like to eat? Are they kind? Are they passionate about their work? Are they success-driven? Are they financially stable? What are their friends and family like? What does "family" mean to them? Do they love children or not so much? What are their best qualities? What are the things you have in common?

For one woman, it took a series of bad relationships before she realized that she was actually asking for all the wrong things. She had grown so tired of overly dramatic and abusive relationships when it finally dawned on her that she was actively attracting all the wrong men. At her lowest point following her most recent breakup, she decided to change that pattern. She began by making a list of the qualities she wanted in her ideal mate. She was very specific, including mutual interests like art, yoga, travel, family, children, and cooking. Most importantly, she

insisted her perfect partner be kind and caring,
and a native New Yorker, just like her.

Soon after, she moved cross-country for work.
While settling in, she decided to take herself along
to a local art gallery. A handsome man walked
in behind her and caught her eye. She worked
up the courage to introduce herself. She soon
discovered that he was a fellow New Yorker who
loved art and travel, and had relocated for work
as a professional chef! They hit it off right away.
The more they got to know each other, the more
the woman was staggered to learn just how many
attributes on her list this man ticked off. To cut a
long story short, a romance blossomed, and they
are now engaged and planning their wedding
back in New York.

Now that you know you can have any type of
romantic partner, and any type of relationship,
and that there are truly no limits, ask yourself
what you *really* want. You do not have to settle for
average or second best. You can have it all, and
you deserve the very best, most wonderful, happy,
and mutually satisfying relationship. So just ask
for it!

Step 2: BELIEVE

Claim the dream relationship you asked for by believing it is already yours. When you do, the Universe will move all circumstances, people, and events for you to receive. And while you wait for your perfect partner to appear, you must *continue to believe.* Have faith. Your belief that the person is already in your life and that you are already in the relationship—that undying faith—is your greatest power.

> *For one young woman, it was her disbelief in love that actually repelled every opportunity she had for romance. Ever since she was a teenager, she had formed the belief that love was only meant for beauty queens. She considered herself a rather plain-looking adolescent, and she had convinced herself that she was destined to remain unlucky in love. The sad irony was that through the years of high school, she had become a very attractive young woman. Yet she continued to see herself as the ugly duckling. Even though heads turned when she walked into a room, nothing could shake her firm belief that she was "not a catch" or the sort of girl a man could fall in love with. A series of failed romances in college only served to reinforce her belief, or rather, her disbelief in love. In each relationship she would fall head over heels*

in love, but within weeks, her worries, fears, and doubts would emerge, and soon she and the young man would break up. She saw this as further proof that she would always be unlucky in love. Of course, the law of attraction says whatever you are thinking and believing about a relationship is exactly what you will receive from that relationship, and so she was destined to continue to experience failed relationships as long as she had thoughts of fear, unworthiness, and bad luck.

After graduation, she secured a job at a firm where, as luck would have it, she worked with a young man she had briefly dated in college. At first, he avoided her and gave the impression that he didn't remember her. When she confronted him, he admitted the reason he was behaving this way was that she had broken his heart when she broke up with him. It had never occurred to her that she was the one sabotaging all of these relationships and her own chances of finding true love. After that realization, she and this young man became very close; they started dating again, and fell deeply in love with one another.

For this woman, it was her long-held belief that she was destined to be unlucky in love that caused her to sabotage every intimate relationship. Once she realized this, she was able to let go of that belief, and only then did she find true love.

Through the law of attraction, your beliefs, true or untrue, form your world.

Step 3: RECEIVE

Perhaps the most important thing you need to do if you want to attract romance is to *feel good*. That's because when you are feeling good, it's much easier to believe you'll receive what you want than if you're not feeling good.

In addition, when you're feeling good, you are on the frequency of all good things coming to you, and you are on the frequency to *receive* what you have asked for.

A story I received from one particular woman is perhaps the best example I have of someone feeling good to receive the perfect person. This woman had lived a very challenging life. She had been married for two decades to an abusive man. His addictions and violent streak condemned the family to poverty in one of the poorest areas of South America. Despite being frequently attacked and beaten by her husband, the woman never complained. Instead, she kept up a happy disposition, especially for her two daughters. Eventually, though, the violence became overwhelming, and she was lucky to escape, taking her two girls with her.

For the next eleven years, the woman remained single, raising teenagers and then putting them through college on her meager earnings. In her part of the world, a woman could not get a decent-paying job or start a career after the age of thirty, but again, this was not something she would complain about. Instead, she spoke optimistically about her dreams: her "new life" overseas, and her new, perfect, handsome husband, a foreigner from America or Europe. She didn't speak of this new life and marriage as a future thing, but as though it was happening now. Her friends and family worried that she was becoming delusional. They thought she had seriously lost it when she started planning an overseas trip and gathered luggage and clothing she would need for the journey. She still didn't have two coins to rub together, yet she applied for a passport and the necessary visas to travel.

The Secret says that if you have an intuitive or instinctive feeling, then you should follow it. What you will find is that the Universe is moving you to receive what you asked for. Well, that's exactly what this woman was doing.

A short time later, a cousin living in Europe invited her over to stay with her and her family. The woman's eldest daughter, who had graduated college by this time and was earning a good living, offered to pay for the flight. She happily accepted. During her travels, she met a wealthy Spanish businessman. He was her perfect handsome foreign man that she had always imagined. He treated her like a princess and they fell madly in love. He invited her back to his home in Spain overlooking the ocean, where they both now live together, happily ever after.

Despite her circumstances, what this woman did was to prepare and to make room to receive her desires. As she did this, she was sending out a powerful signal of belief and expectation, and the Universe was perfectly happy to oblige.

If you want to meet your perfect partner, make sure your actions are reflecting what you expect to receive. What does that mean? It means doing what you would do if you were in that relationship *now*.

What actions can you take that say you have already received your perfect partner or perfect relationship? For instance:

- Are you doing all you can to look and feel
  your best?
- Do you keep the front passenger seat of your
  car clean and uncluttered for your perfect
  partner to sit when you go out on a date?
- Is there room in your closet for your perfect
  partner's clothes?
- How about setting the table for two people
  instead of one?
- Or making room in your bed by sleeping on
  one side instead of in the middle, and putting
  out two toothbrushes in the bathroom?

There's no end to the creative ways that you
can take specific actions that will guarantee you
receive what you've asked for.

And when you are truly ready to receive, the law
of attraction will use circumstances, events, and
people to bring the perfect relationship to you.

So follow the Creative Process for the relationship
you want to attract. Don't waver from your belief,
and do your best to feel as good as you can. And
then nothing can get in the way of the Universe
delivering to you what you asked for.

LESSON 5

IMAGINATION AND RELATIONSHIPS

Your entire life is what you have imagined it to be. Whether you're aware of it or not, everything you have or don't have, every situation and circumstance, and every relationship within your life is what you have imagined it to be. The problem is that many people imagine the worst! They're turning the most wonderful tool against themselves. Instead of imagining the best, many people are in fear and imagine all the things that can go wrong. And as surely as they keep imagining and feeling those things, they happen. Think about and imagine the best you can in your relationships, because the best you can imagine is a piece of cake for the law of attraction!

Remember, life isn't happening to you; life is *responding* to you. Life is your call! Every area of your life is your call. Whether you want a perfect partner, a better marriage, or a better relationship with your boss, simply get yourself onto the receiving frequency. You do that by imagining and feeling what it would be like to have that relationship.

When you imagine anything that you want and love, you are harnessing the law of attraction. As you imagine something positive, such as a caring, loving relationship, and you feel good as you imagine it, then that is what you'll receive. Your thoughts, desire, and feelings create the magnetism, the magnetic power, drawing what you want to you. If you can imagine it, through thinking and feeling it, then you can receive it.

But you have to make sure to use your imagination for what you want rather than for what you don't want. This is the difference between someone who is struggling in life and someone who has a fabulous life. Those who have a great life imagine what they want, and they feel the good feelings of what they're imagining.

People who are struggling are unintentionally using their imagination for what they don't want, and are feeling the negativity of what they're imagining. It's such a simple thing, but it creates vast differences in people's lives.

Therefore, if you want to attract the perfect relationship, imagine that relationship exactly the way you want it to be. Then, all you need to do is feel the feelings of being in that relationship right now.

One woman took this advice about imagination and wrote a letter to her future husband, thanking him for treating her so well. She was grateful for all of his wonderful qualities, for his kindness and humor, and for their shared interests, such as classical music, travel, art, and reading. She went on to describe a romantic date that they had shared. She hadn't even met this mystery man, yet she described their life together in great detail. You won't be surprised to learn that she met her perfect partner a short time later, and he turned out to be exactly as she described in her letter. And the location he took her on their first date? Exactly the place she had imagined and written about.

The Powerful Process of Visualization

Whatever you can imagine is waiting for you, fully created in the invisible. The way to make it visible is to harness the law of attraction by picturing it in your mind and feeling as if you already have what you want right now. This process is known as visualization.

The reason visualization is so powerful is because you are creating pictures in your mind that make you feel that you already have what you want. Visualization is simply powerfully focused thought in pictures, and it causes equally powerful feelings. When you are imagining something or visualizing something, you are emitting that powerful frequency out into the Universe. The law of attraction will take hold of that signal and return those pictures back to you as your life, just as you saw them in your mind.

To visualize a relationship, simply close your eyes and picture having the sort of relationship that you want. As you imagine doing all the things you want to do in this relationship, you are creating a new reality. Your subconscious mind and the law of attraction do not know whether you are imagining something or whether it is real. And when you are in the place where the relationship you are imagining feels real—when you believe it—you will know that it has penetrated your subconscious mind. And the law of attraction must deliver.

The key to visualizing relationships or anything else you want is to keep the pictures moving in your mind, and yourself moving in the picture. If you keep the pictures moving like a movie, you can master visualization really quickly. If the picture is static, it is a lot harder to hold the picture in your mind. Besides, relationships are not static, they are active and dynamic. So keep your visualization busy with lots of movement, lots of activity, and of course, lots of conversation. Your mind will become so captivated by the moving pictures, it will not be able to think of anything else.

When you use visualization, picture every scene and situation you can with the relationship you want, and feel that you have it now. Imagine and feel the love and gratitude for having it. Do this each day until you feel as though you already have your desire. Do it until you know that relationship belongs to you, just as you know your name belongs to you. You might get to this state after just one or two days, or it may take you longer. Then simply get on with your life, having as many good thoughts and good feelings as you can. That's because the more good thoughts and feelings you have, the more you are on the receiving frequency, and the faster you will receive all that will make you feel good!

Using visualization to create your dream life is very much like making a movie of your life. In fact, you are creating the movie of your life right now. So how is the movie of your life going? Do you need to make any script changes, perhaps in how your characters relate to each other? Maybe you'd like a casting change or to add a romantic lead? Is there any editing that you want to do? Today is the day to use your imagination to make any changes that you want to your life movie, because today's visualized changes will be screening tomorrow.

Vision Boards

Another way to harness your imagination to attract amazing relationships is with a *Vision Board*. You can let your imagination go wild with a Vision Board, by placing pictures of all the things you want, and pictures of how you want your life to be.

As you look at the Vision Board, you are imprinting the images in your mind. As you focus on your Vision Board, it stimulates your senses and evokes positive thoughts and feelings within you. Then you have the two elements of creation—your mind and your feelings—working in full force.

Whatever it is you want, look for pictures of those things and place them on your Vision Board. For instance, you can find pictures of a couple in love, a group of friends, a happy family, children, a newborn baby, or someone on a holiday abroad with a friend or partner. You can use photographs of yourself next to pictures of a dream partner to help you imagine your ideal relationship.

I know of one woman who broke the cycle of failed romantic relationships with the aid of a Vision Board. She had basically been single for the better part of a decade. Dating was one disappointment after another. So she turned to a Vision Board as somewhat of a last resort. She gathered typical pictures of couples in love—kissing, dancing, hugging, and generally being romantic. She added in words of hope and optimism, such as "future husband," "the love of my life," and "romance." When she went on dates, even if they didn't work out, she remained hopeful and appreciative of the fact that she was one step closer to her perfect

*partner. And she was right. When he finally
appeared, she was ready. They fell in love and
they are now planning their future lives together.
All because of a Vision Board.*

Make sure you put your Vision Board in a place
where you see it and look at it every day. *Feel* the
feelings of having those things now. The more
you feel it and believe it, the faster the things will
manifest.

Journaling

Writing or journaling is another great way to use
your imagination for incredible relationships.

If you want to attract the perfect partner into
your life, you can describe in writing exactly
what that person is like, and what your
relationship is like. You can include their likes,
dislikes, tastes, hobbies, family background,
profession, and anything else important to you.
You should be able to create a list of at least
one hundred things that describe your perfect
partner. And then just sit back and watch how
the Universe orchestrates a person matching
your description into your life.

*One young man awoke from a particularly vivid
dream convinced that he had just met the love
of his life. He described her as Asian, with long,
black hair, and much shorter than he was. When
he told his friends that he had seen his future
wife in his dream, they laughed. But to him,
it was no joke. However, years passed with no
sign of the girl, and he began to lose hope. Then
she returned to him in another dream. This
time, he caught her name—Ayu. He decided
to write a story about a man who was visited
by the girl of his dreams. He called the story
"Dream Girl" and he described his heroine in
great detail, naming her Ayu after his own
dream girl.*

*A short time later, he was casually navigating
a social media website when he chanced upon
the profile of an Asian woman who looked
remarkably familiar. Her profile was locked,
which meant he had no way to contact her, so he
just moved on. Besides, her name was not Ayu.
A few days later, this very same woman sent
him a friend request. She had seen his profile too,
and felt compelled to get in touch. They made an
instant connection, and soon fell in love. And
would you believe it—her middle name was Ayu!
He had not only dreamed his dream girl, he had
written her into his life.*

Play Make-Believe

Another way you can use your imagination to transform your relationships is to create games in your mind, and to play.

At some point, we stopped playing and having fun like we did as children, with the result that as we became adults, we became more serious about life. But seriousness brings serious circumstances into your life. When you play and have fun, you feel really good, and—voilà—really good circumstances come into your life.

The point is, life is supposed to be fun. Play with the law of attraction, and invent games with your imagination, because the law of attraction doesn't care if you're imagining and playing, or if it is real. Whatever you imagine and feel will become real!

How do you play? You do the same thing as you did when you were a child, and you use your imagination to create make-believe games.

When you were a child playing make-believe, do you remember how convincing your imagination was to you? Well, this is what you must do when you want to manifest anything. Secretly, inside yourself, pretend that you have what you want already. For example, if you want great friendships, make believe or pretend that you have great friends now. The moment you tip the balance by imagining and feeling that you have great friends now *more* than noticing that you don't, you will have great friends. This simple formula applies to everything.

If you want a romantic relationship, then make believe that you have it now. Play! Pretend that you are on a blind date with your perfect partner— what would that look like? If you just met the love of your life, how would you feel? You would feel different from how you feel now. Everything about you would change. You would walk differently, you would talk differently, and you would act as though you were on top of the world. Walk like that now! Talk like that now! Act as if you have it now!

Whatever it is you want, use your imagination, create games, and play. Do whatever you can to generate the feeling that you have what you want already. Surround yourself with items of clothing, pictures, photographs, and objects relevant to what you want to create. Use every prop you can find to help you, so you can imagine and feel the feelings of having the relationship that you want.

A truly incredible example of this came from a young single mother who had been alone and looking for love for over three years. One day, she was in the city trying to find a particular street when a wedding dress in a shop window caught her eye. She went inside to take a closer look. The shop assistant encouraged her to try it on, and against all common sense or reason, she wound up buying that dress. To be clear, she had no significant other, and so no wedding plans or need for a wedding dress. Outside the shop, she bumped into a man who looked very familiar. He was the spitting image of an actor she liked, and whose face adorned her computer as a screen saver. In one of those stranger-than-fiction coincidences, he just happened to be looking for the same address that she was, and so they set off in search of it together. Needless to say, they hit it off immediately, and soon began dating. Within months, they had moved in together, and they are now happily married. Incredibly, this woman attracted her husband with the help of a computer screen saver, and the powerful action of buying a wedding dress.

No matter how you use your imagination to attract new and better relationships, the important thing is to feel good when you're visualizing. Capture that energy as you imagine your ideal relationship. Quick flashes of imagining and feeling your desire are all you need to harness the power of your thoughts and feelings for what you want! This is playing. This is fun. This is the joy of creating your life.

LESSON 6

GRATITUDE AND RELATIONSHIPS

Ancient spiritual traditions teach us that when we are grateful to others with a full heart it enriches our lives in ways we can barely fathom. Science confirms this, with research studies showing that people who practice gratitude have closer relationships and are more connected to family and friends and the wider community. The research also shows that those practicing gratitude are more optimistic and positive about their current lives as well as their future.

When you are grateful, you're happy, and you become a magnet to happy people, happy situations, and happy events in your life. Gratitude is the bridge from misery to happiness, and from despair and loneliness to a life filled with love, joy, and amazing relationships.

I know of thousands of people in the worst imaginable situations who have changed their lives completely through gratitude. I know of broken relationships transformed into magnificent ones, failed marriages completely restored, estranged family members reunited, and parents' relationships with children and teenagers transformed.

If you use gratitude a little, your relationships and your life will change a little. If you use gratitude a lot, every day, your relationships and your life will change in ways you can hardly imagine now.

Whether you're giving thanks to a person, or feeling grateful for a gift, a sunset, a shared experience, or a new relationship, by the law of attraction you will receive back more joy, more gifts, more amazing experiences, and more love in your relationships.

An Exercise in Gratitude

Try this now. Think of someone you're grateful for. You could choose the person you love more than anyone else in the world. Or you can choose someone you're having difficulties with. Focus on that person and think about all the things you love and are grateful for about that person. Then, in your mind or out loud, tell that person all those things you love and are grateful for about them, as though they were with you. Tell them all the reasons you love them. You can recall particular instances or moments by saying, "I remember the time when . . ." (and then fill in the blank). As you're doing it, feel the gratitude begin to fill your heart and body.

The love and gratitude you feel in this simple exercise must and will return to you in the relationship, and in your whole life. That is how easy it is to change your life through gratitude.

I know of one woman who had experienced a strained relationship with her mother for much of her life. While there had been some heated arguments in the past, it was really more a case that they were just very different people who expected different things in a relationship. The mother was quite reserved and the daughter was more affectionate. As a result, they were never close, and over time, they had simply stopped communicating altogether. Then, as the mother grew older and began to lose her eyesight, the daughter felt the need to reassess their relationship and possibly reconnect.

The first thing she did was to reflect back to when she was growing up, and to make a list of all the things she was grateful for that her mother had done. For instance, there were the dresses that her mother sewed for her. Then there were the vegetables that her mother grew for the family and the large garden that she tended, and the years of hard work and caring. The younger woman gave thanks for all of it, and then made plans to visit her mother.

When they met, everything had changed. The usual tension was gone, and it was replaced by love and happiness. The mother even offered her daughter a warm hug for the first time ever. They committed to regular contact and a new trusting and supportive relationship. The relationship that the daughter had always dreamed of having with her mother finally came true.

Gratitude begins with two simple words—*thank you*—but to make it really powerful you have to feel grateful with all your heart. The more you say *thank you*, the more you will feel it, and the faster you will see the results in your life.

How to Use Gratitude

There are three ways to use the power of gratitude in your life:

The first is to be grateful for what you have received in the past.

The second is to be grateful for everything you are receiving or have now.

And the third way to use the power of gratitude is to be grateful for what you *want*, as though you have received it already.

When you are grateful for a past relationship, the appreciation and gratitude that you feel improves your relationships and attracts new ones that you will be grateful for.

When you are grateful for a current relationship, even if it's not perfect, the relationship will get better.

And when you are grateful for relationships you want in the future, and you give thanks as though they are already a part of your life, then they will surely materialize.

Gratitude for your relationships—past, present, and future—attracts into your life more love and happiness than you could ever imagine. That's because gratitude is the great multiplier of life! When you give thanks for what you've received and what you're continuing to receive, it *multiplies* those things. At the same time, gratitude brings what you want! When you are grateful for what you want, as though you have received it, the law of attraction says you *must* receive it.

And if you're not grateful for what you've received and what you're receiving, you don't have the power to change any of your current circumstances.

Taking Things for Granted

When we are not grateful for each thing in our lives, we are unintentionally taking all that we have for granted. Taking our relationships for granted can cause a lot of negativity in our life. That's because when we take relationships or people for granted, we are unintentionally taking from ourselves. The law of attraction says that like attracts like, so if we take anyone or anything for granted, we will be taken from as a result.

Ask yourself:

Are you only grateful for your friends when you need them? Do you take them for granted most of the time?

Are you only grateful for your loved ones when everything is going well? Do you only talk about your relationships when there are problems?

Are you grateful to your parents for the life they've given you, or do you take your life for granted?

Just as giving thanks will always lead to the things we are grateful for multiplying, so must taking things for granted lead to us losing the things we take for granted.

If you can, be grateful for everything in your life, and take nothing and no one for granted. Be grateful for your loved ones, your friends, your child, your pet . . . for your ability to love and be loved. Compliment people wherever you go. Be a ray of sunshine to everyone you meet, and make their day better for having seen you. Say thank you at every turn. Walk, talk, think, and breathe appreciation. When you do this, you will have locked into the frequency of gratitude, and all good things will be yours.

Research studies have found that when the average person is thanked for their service, they want to do even more for the person who thanked them. And the results are even stronger when they involve spouses or partners. When a spouse responds with gratitude to an act of kindness from their partner, the partner is motivated to perform even more acts of kindness. This inspires even more gratitude and acts of kindness from the spouse until it snowballs into a cycle of kindness and gratitude. It's the perfect demonstration of the law of attraction in action. And all it takes to maintain that cycle is a little gratitude.

Gratitude for Difficult Relationships

You can improve any difficult or negative relationship through the use of gratitude. You do this simply by looking for things you love

and appreciate in the other person. This may
seem challenging at first, especially if you have
harbored bad feelings for that person for quite
some time. Make a deliberate effort to constantly
look for things you appreciate and are grateful for
in the other person. When you do this, you will
be astounded at what happens. It will appear to
you as though something incredible has happened
to the other person. But it's your gratitude that
is incredible, because it dissolves negativity,
including negativity in relationships. All you have
to do is be grateful for that person, and everything
will change in the relationship!

*For one man, his most difficult relationship was
with a short-tempered colleague who had become
his team leader. It was a small team of six, and it
seemed as though every day one of them would
come under intense scrutiny from the team leader.
They would receive fierce lectures for every little
mistake. He would rant and rave, throw pens
and papers, and he would escalate every minor
issue right up the chain to senior management.
At first the man was able to avoid the ire of his
team leader. But gradually he felt himself become
the target of his boss's unresolved anger. He
came to dread the daily verbal abuse. He became
depressed, and he even started to question his
value as an employee and as a person.*

Then, he decided to switch things up. He stopped thinking and worrying about his team leader's next temper tantrum, and he took measures to change the whole nature of their relationship. From that point on, whenever he received any verbal abuse or criticism, he would respond to the team leader by thanking him for correcting his mistakes. He would tell the team leader that he was grateful for the help to make him a better worker and more valued employee. He would also compliment the leader on his excellent leadership skills and other attributes. The results were almost instantaneous. The scolding criticism and complaints stopped, and for the first time ever, the team leader thanked the man for his work. He even began to talk to the man as though they were old friends. Nothing really changed with the team leader for other members of the team, and they continued to receive harsh lectures. But at least this man was able to dramatically improve his own work situation.

There is gold in every one of your relationships, even those that may be difficult or appear to be filled with negativity. To bring riches to all your relationships and your life, you have to find the gold.

Gratitude for Failed Relationships

It is also possible to salvage gold from the wreckage of any failed relationship by practicing gratitude.

If you find yourself in this situation, think back through the history of the failed relationship, and list all the things you're grateful for about the person. The easiest way to do this is to think back to the way things were *before* the relationship deteriorated or ended. If the relationship was never good, then think hard about any good qualities in the person, or the great things you learned from the relationship.

For example, if you have an ex-partner who is connected to you through your children, and the relationship isn't good, look at your children's faces. Realize that they wouldn't be alive if it wasn't for your ex-partner. Your children's lives are one of the most precious gifts you have. Look at your children, and give thanks to your ex-partner for their lives every single day! As well as bringing peace and harmony to the relationship, through your example you will be teaching your children the greatest tool for their life—gratitude.

As you reflect upon a failed relationship, keep in mind that this exercise is not about who is right or wrong. It doesn't matter what you feel someone has done to you, what someone said or how it may have hurt you. *You* can heal the relationship, and you don't need the other person in order to heal it. It only takes one person to change a relationship through gratitude, but it is the person who uses gratitude who receives the benefits in their whole life.

> *From the time one woman was just a little girl, the only father she knew was an alcoholic, drug-addicted, abusive man who was in and out of prison her whole life. As a child and teenager, she blamed herself for the lack of love he had shown her. Even as a grown woman, she wondered who would ever love her when her own father could not. Eventually she came to realize that she had to forgive him in order to move on with her life. She wished him well wherever he was, and she gave thanks that he had taught her what type of parent and person she wanted to be. Through his example, she had come to see that she wanted to protect and cherish the people she loved, and to help them in any way she could to make them happy. By choosing to practice gratitude, she is now well on the way to achieving her dream — with a loving husband, three beautiful children, and a wonderful life.*

When you make a deliberate effort to be grateful for all of the relationships in your life, both past and present, a miracle will take place. From that positive state of pure gratitude, you will experience the most peaceful sense of relief and closure over any past conflict or dysfunction. You will also find that your current relationships will improve dramatically, and you will welcome new and fulfilling relationships into your life. You will say goodbye to fear, worry, grief, and depression. And in their place will be happiness, clarity, patience, kindness, compassion, understanding, and peace of mind. Such is the power of gratitude.

LESSON 7

THE SECRET TO YOU

It can often be the case that we are critical of ourselves and don't love ourselves completely. To not love ourselves can keep what we want *from* us when we are seeking love in our life. When we don't love ourselves, we are literally pushing the love that we want away from us.

Unless you fill yourself up first, you have nothing to give anybody. If you want to attract new or better relationships, it is imperative that you tend to *you* first. If you don't treat yourself with love and respect, you are sending out a signal to the Universe that says you are not worthy enough or deserving of love. That signal will continue to be broadcast, and you will experience more situations of people not treating you with love and respect. The people are just the effect. Your thoughts are the cause.

Critical thoughts about yourself cause the greatest harm to your life, because they make you feel really bad. And then wherever you go and whatever you do, you take those negative feelings with you in every moment. Those feelings taint everything you touch; they taint the way you perceive the world, and they affect all the circumstances of your life. Negative thoughts about yourself act as a magnet, attracting more dissatisfaction, discontentment, and disappointment with everything you do.

Changing the Way You Think of Yourself

You can begin to change how you feel by changing the way you think of yourself. And when you do that, the law of attraction will move the entire

Universe to match what you are emitting, and your life will be full of people who love and respect you.

I know of one woman who struggled to feel comfortable in any social situation because she didn't think well of herself. In fact, she had come to feel so unworthy of attention that no matter where she went or who she was with, she always felt "outshone" by others. In her mind, she was everyone else's afterthought, confined to the shadows. Though she knew she was selling herself short, she simply couldn't stop believing that she was not good enough. Her love life suffered, with every relationship doomed to failure due to her thoughts of unworthiness.

It was only when she decided to change her way of thinking that her circumstances began to change. Instead of being outshone, she decided that she would shine. She decided that she would turn heads when she walked down the street or when she entered a room. She told herself over and over again that she was more than good enough. She began to appreciate herself and value herself, and believe that she deserved nothing but the best. And with this newfound confidence came the greatest feeling of happiness. Of course, the law of attraction inevitably responded to those good thoughts and feelings, and the woman soon met the love of her life. She says she hasn't stopped smiling since the day they met, and she doubts she ever will.

This woman stopped entertaining thoughts of unworthiness, and began to think more positively about herself. She discovered that the more she focused on feeling good about herself, the more good things came into her life, including her perfect partner. She came to learn that you have to be rich with good, positive thoughts and feelings about yourself to bring the riches of life to you. In fact, it is impossible to be truly happy if you don't love you. And if you don't love yourself, you are blocking all the love and all the good that the Universe has for you.

Falling in Love With You

To create the life of your dreams, including wonderful relationships and unshakable happiness, the time has come for you to fall in love with you. Falling in love with you is not about arrogance or conceit, but about a healthy love and respect for yourself—just as you are. When you love yourself, you become a magnet of love, and you will attract more love in your relationships and more of the things you love in every area of your life. Fall in love with you so that the rest of the world can love you too.

So how do you fall in love with you?

You fall in love with you the same way you fall in love with another person—you adore *everything* about them! When you fall in love with another person, you see only love, hear only love, speak only love, and *feel* love with all your heart. So fall in love with *you* by looking for all the good things about you, and by doing all the things that make *you* feel good.

And wherever you are in your day, whatever you're doing, look for the things you love. Think about what you love. Talk about what you love. Do what you love to do and do it with a passion until your heart is full to overflowing. When you love whatever you do as much as you can, it helps attract people you love, relationships you love, and all the things that you love back to you. A heart on fire with passion is the most attractive force in the Universe.

A bride-to-be was practically left at the altar by her fiancé, who dumped her unceremoniously for another woman. Heartbroken and with a plummeting sense of self-worth, she spent the

next two years trying to use The Secret to win
him back. This was doomed to fail, as his free will
was to be with someone else. Eventually she let
him go, and made the decision to seek her true
love. To do that, she realized she had to learn to
love herself and to actually start enjoying life, so
that the Universe could deliver the perfect partner
to her. First, she found a new passion—rock
climbing. The joy she felt for this new activity
filled her heart to overflowing. So it's no surprise
that rock climbing was what ended up bringing
her together with the new love of her life—a
fellow rock climber. And now, after two years of
dating, rock climbing, and scaling mountains
together, she feels quite literally on top of the
world.

Happiness Attracts Happiness

Your job is to love as much as possible every
day. Love and adore everything you possibly can
today, including yourself, and turn away from
the things you don't love. If you can just do that,
your tomorrows will overflow with the untold
happiness of everything you love.

For many people, this will come across as
counterintuitive. They will wonder how they are

supposed to love when they feel utterly unloved. But it can be no other way. In order to receive love, first you must love. In order to receive untold happiness, first you must be happy.

And right there is one of the great secrets behind The Secret.

In fact, it's the shortcut to anything you want in your life:

BE and FEEL happy now!

It is the fastest way to attract love, happy relationships, and anything else you want into your life. Focus on radiating out into the Universe those thoughts and feelings of joy and happiness. When you do that, you will attract back to you more things that bring you joy and happiness.

Unfortunately, most of us have the wrong idea about happiness. We believe that once we get everything we want, we will be happy.

But if you have been living your life saying to yourself, "I will be happy when I find true love," or "I will be happy when my divorce comes through," or "I will be happy when I meet some new friends," or "I will be happy when problems with my family are resolved," or "I will be happy when my boss respects me," then you will never have those things, because your thoughts are defying the way life works. They're defying the law of attraction.

You have to be happy *first* to receive happy things! You have to fill yourself with happiness in order to attract happy circumstances, happy people, and happy relationships. It can't happen any other way, because whatever you want to *receive* in life, you must think and feel first!

It's a simple formula . . . *Happiness attracts happiness.*

People use so many excuses as to why they can't be happy, and why they can't use this simple formula, but it is law: be happy now and you will attract even more things that will make you happy.

Being Happy Despite Your Circumstances

Unless you begin to feel happy despite your life circumstances, then you cannot attract more happiness or happy relationships. The law of attraction says, be happy now, and as long as you keep doing that, you will receive unlimited happiness and a life full of things that make you happy.

One woman held a lifelong dream of marrying and having a happy, healthy, loving family and a home of her own. However, after getting married, she and her husband were saddled with his prior debts. In addition, they each suffered mild bouts of depression, and so they agreed to put off having children. As time wore on, that promise of a happy family life and home just seemed to slip further and further away. Then, after ten years together, the husband left and this woman's dreams of happiness appeared to be shattered forever.

Surviving heartbreak and a difficult divorce, she went on a journey of self-love, and found solace in yoga, the saving grace of her life. She also began to dote on her nieces and nephews. It wasn't quite the same as having a family of her own, but it would do. Mind you, she never completely let go of her lifelong dream. She still pictured her home, and she imagined her perfect partner—loving and kind, debt-free, and owning his own graphic-design business in her hometown. As you can see, her wish list was quite specific. Nevertheless, she got on with living the single life and became truly happy within herself.

*Not long after, she met someone online, who she
soon discovered matched up with her wish list
right down to the smallest detail. He was very
loving and kind, ran a graphic design firm, and
owned his own home that looked very much like
the one she'd always dreamed about. They fell in
love and they have since become engaged. They
are planning a family, and living a happier life
than the woman could have ever dreamed possible.*

*But of course, this happiness didn't come from
getting married, having a family, or living in
her dream home—quite the contrary. It was only
when this woman was able to fill herself with
happiness regardless of what was going on in her
life that she was able to attract a happy marriage,
a family, a home, and a life filled with happiness.*

Your life is in your hands. No matter what has
happened in the past, you can now consciously
choose a life that is filled with happiness.
Happiness comes from giving your full attention
to the thoughts that make you feel happy and
ignoring thoughts that don't make you feel
happy. When you give your attention to thoughts
that make you feel happy, not only will you be
happier, but every circumstance in your life will
improve! Happiness and love are like two sides of
a coin. You can't have happiness without giving
and feeling love.

Regardless of how many mistakes you've made, regardless of where you are in your life, and regardless of what *you* think of you, the Universe is completely and utterly in love with you. And when you begin to love yourself, then the love of others will most certainly find you.

LESSON 8

THE GREATEST GIFT

According to the law of attraction, in every circumstance and moment of your life, you are receiving back whatever you have given out, whether you make the connection or not. Quite simply, you get what you give.

It makes sense that if it's love and appreciation you want, then love and appreciation are what you must give.

Every single day, no matter who you meet—friends, family, work colleagues, even strangers—you have endless opportunities to give love and appreciation to them. Giving a smile or a compliment, a kind word or a kind action, or even just privately feeling love in your heart for someone—each is an example of giving love and appreciation.

When you feel happy, it is your guarantee that you will be giving positivity and love to whomever you come into contact with. This is true even if you connect with a person just briefly in a store, on a bus, in an elevator, or even on the phone. When your good feelings make a difference to any person you connect with, the effect of that one instance on *your* life is almost incomprehensible. When you give love and appreciation to anyone, the love will return to you, but in a far greater way than you may have realized.

When you give love to another person, and your love affects the other person positively, they can then pass that love on to someone else. No matter how many people are positively affected, no matter how far the effect of your love travels, *all* that love comes back to *you*. And the love returns to you dressed as circumstances, people, and events that you love in your life.

One young woman used this practice to heal a broken heart and meet the love of her life. Prior to this, she had been going through a roller coaster of emotions due to an on-again, off-again intimate relationship over the course of three years. In the last year alone, her boyfriend had broken up with her four times. It wasn't that he didn't love her, but he did have problems with commitment. And while she was certain that he never intended to hurt her, his insecurities and indecision caused her a tremendous amount of heartache. On the final instance of their breaking up, she commenced a practice that she'd read about in my book The Magic. *The practice involves giving love to others without expectation of return. They then share that love with others, who share it with others, and it continues on as a chain of love, which returns to you in the most unexpected ways.*

The woman launched into the practice by volunteering to help people struggling with depression and anxiety. Coincidentally, in the course of volunteering, she met a man who was kind, compassionate, and perfect in so many ways. They bonded immediately, and despite the fact that she was not necessarily looking for love, a new relationship blossomed. Simply by giving her time and her love and compassion to so many others, she received more love and compassion than she could ever have dreamed of.

That's when her ex returned, begging her forgiveness and insisting that he was a changed man. He even got down on one knee and proposed marriage. From her perspective, he seemed completely genuine. She felt that he had truly changed and become the man she had longed for ever since their very first breakup. But she held firm. She gently rejected his proposal, and wished him well.

Meanwhile, she committed herself to her new relationship with the man of her dreams, enjoying the type of loving relationship that she had never imagined was possible.

Giving from a Full Heart

One of the most powerful practices is giving without any expectation of receiving. When you give from a full heart, the law of attraction will grab hold of that signal and return the love back to you in your life.

You'll also find that giving from a full heart is one of the most joyous things you can do, because you are giving the very best of you! You are giving your true nature, which is love.

Indeed, our highest power is love, and it is the one thing each of us has an unlimited amount of.

No human being has a lesser amount, nor does
anyone have limits on the amount of love they
can bring forth from within them. Each day we
have an opportunity to set out with this great,
unlimited power in our possession, and give it out
to every person we come in contact with.

How much love do *you* give to others in one day?

Giving love is appreciating, complimenting, feeling
gratitude, giving a smile, and speaking kind words
to others. You can give courtesy to other motorists
while you are driving. You can give a smile to
the car parking attendant. You can give a warm
greeting to the shop clerk or to the person who
makes your coffee. You can give love by allowing
a stranger to go ahead of you into an elevator,
and you can give love by asking which floor they
are going to and pressing the button for them. If
someone drops something, you can give a helping
hand and pick it up for them. You can give warm
embraces to those you love. And you can give
appreciation and encouragement to everyone.

We Are One

When we give love, it returns to us because we are
One. We are all connected, and we are all part of

the One Energy Field, or the One Supreme Mind, or the One Consciousness, or the One Creative Source. Call it whatever you want, but we are all One.

If you think about the law of attraction now, in terms of us all being One, you will see its absolute perfection.

And you will understand why your negative thoughts about someone else will return to harm only you.

When you call upon the law of attraction to ask for something for yourself, try also asking for everyone. Good things for you—good things for everyone. Prosperity for you—prosperity for everyone. Health for you—health for everyone. Joy for you—and joy for everyone. Love, happiness, and harmonious relationships for you—love, happiness, and harmonious relationships for everyone in the world.

Can you imagine what would happen if billions of people asked for these things for you?

It's a small thing you can do that has incredible results.

A middle-aged woman regarded giving to others as her favorite thing to do. However, her whole world was shaken to its core when in a short period of time she experienced a number of tragic circumstances. First, her sister died of cancer, then her brother was killed in an accident, and then her mother passed away after a long illness. On top of all that, her marriage crumbled after thirty-nine years. Nevertheless, she overcame her misery with dreams of a better future in which she would help to make the world a better place. Her greatest dream was to teach and help children through her love of music and horse riding.

Throughout her family's traumatic time, her son had been begging her to come visit him at his home in Costa Rica. Once her divorce was finalized, she agreed, especially as she now had a brand-new baby grandson to meet. She fell in love with Costa Rica right away, not just for the climate and lifestyle, but for the opportunity it gave her. She was able to teach English to local children as well as offer guitar lessons and horse riding—just as she had always dreamed. She also met the man of her dreams; he owned horses, and they went on to marry and settle in his beautiful home right there in Costa Rica. But of course, this was simply all the giving returning to a woman whose greatest desire had always been to give to others.

Give your love because it is the magnet to *all* the riches of life. And your life will become richer than you thought was possible, because when you give love, you are fulfilling the entire purpose of your life. When you give love, you will receive back so much love and joy that you will feel it is almost more than you can take. But you *can* take unlimited love and joy, because that is what you are, and because loving is the purpose of your life.

Giving love is the ultimate pathway to be in complete harmony with the law of attraction. In fact, the law of attraction has been called the law of love, because the law itself is a gift of love to humanity. It is the law by which we can create incredible lives for ourselves. The more love we give, the greater our power to create a magnificent life of love, joy, and harmony.

A Summary of

The Secret to Love

Your relationships are in your hands. It doesn't matter what state your relationships are in now, nor does it matter what has happened up to this point. You can begin to consciously choose your thoughts, and you can change any relationship in your life, or attract any new one you desire. You are here on this glorious planet, endowed with this wonderful power to create your whole life. There are no limits to what you can create for you, because your ability to think good thoughts is unlimited. Harmony in relationships, happiness, and love will come to you in the future based on your thoughts today.

Remember though, you create for yourself through your thoughts, but you cannot create other people's lives for them. You cannot think for them, and if you try to force your opinions or impose your will on others, you will only attract the same being done to you. Imposing your will is when you do not allow someone else the freedom to be as they are. Imposing your will can also result in you attracting negative situations or events where you find yourself powerless.

So let all others create the life they want, let them do what they want, to be with who they want, and to love whoever they want.

This can be tough, as many brokenhearted people who have written to me will attest.

However, if you find yourself in this situation, it's not all doom and gloom. Whether you are suffering from a broken heart, or unrequited love, or feelings of loneliness, there is a silver lining.

You see, it's the heartbreak from challenging times that gives us the greatest desire to change things in our life. That huge desire for your life to be better is like a magnetic fire, and it is very powerful. Be grateful for everything that caused that fire to ignite the desire within you. That burning desire will give you strength and determination, and you *will* change your life.

Everything in life is presenting itself to you so you can choose what you want and what you don't want. Life is like a catalogue. You are the one who chooses from the catalogue, by giving your attention and your thoughts to that thing! Life's catalogue contains many things you don't want, so be careful not to inadvertently choose them by thinking about them. Only thoughts of what you want bring what you want to you!

So when you see a happy couple madly in love, and you desperately want a partner in your life, feel good about the happy couple. Life's catalogue is presenting the happy couple to you so you can choose it. If you feel sad or lonely when you see the happy couple, the law of attraction receives, "I want to be sad and lonely," because that is what you focused on. You have to think about what you want in order to receive what you want.

When you feel good about anything any person has, you are bringing it to you. When you feel good about the success of another person, the happiness of another person, or all the good things anyone else has, you are choosing those things from the catalogue of life for you.

If you meet someone who has qualities you wish you had, love those qualities in that person, and you are bringing those qualities to yourself. If someone is smart, beautiful, or talented, love those qualities and you choose those things for *you*!

When you see that happy couple, friends enjoying each other's company, children laughing, or a potential partner, it means you are on the same frequency as that thing! Be happy, because your happiness is choosing it. Your happiness is drawing it to you.

You came into this world to create the life you want. Your mind is your powerful tool to bring whatever you want to you, if you would just give your attention only to the thoughts of what you want! It is easy to be positive, to be grateful, to appreciate, and to give love, because those things fill you with pure positive energy and good feelings. And it takes so much energy from us when we are negative, critical, and take things for granted.

Your life is in your hands, as it is for everyone. One thought can change everything! You can be, do, or have whatever you want. You can have the relationship of your dreams with everyone in your life through consistent thoughts of appreciation, gratitude, and love.

May the joy be with you.

Rhonda Byrne

THE SECRET
TO HEALTH

INTRODUCTION

THE SECRET TO HEALTH

We should feel like we're overflowing with good health, energy, and happiness most of the time, because that is our birthright. The reality, however, is that a lot of people don't feel this way very often, if ever. Many people are dealing with illnesses, problems with the functioning of their body, or suffering from bouts of depression and other mental-health problems, which are all states of less than full health.

Perfect health is our birthright and every one of us deserves it, but if that's the case, why don't we all have it? There are multiple reasons for a lack of health, but the primary reason that affects the majority of the population is that we are using the power of our mind toward illness and disease, instead of toward health and well-being.

Ancient spiritual teachings tell us that the health of our body is completely governed by the subconscious mind, and as you will discover, simply knowing that makes it easy to reprogram your body toward health.

Throughout our life we have programmed our subconscious mind with many beliefs. Whatever thought we believe to be true goes straight into the subconscious mind as a belief, and from there it must appear in our life, mirroring that belief. What we believe will always come true in our life—unless we change the belief.

When you came into this world, your subconscious mind was a clean slate, but gradually over the years you have absorbed the opinions, viewpoints, perspectives, and beliefs of your parents, teachers, friends, and society. Many of the beliefs you've accepted into your subconscious got there in your very early childhood years. We don't have the capacity to discern at an early age, and so we tend to accept everything that is told to us by adults.

There are some beliefs that serve you; positive beliefs such as "I know I can do anything I set my mind to." But in the area of health, many people carry around beliefs that do not serve them; beliefs about allergies, or catching colds easily, or certain diseases that they believe run in their family. Unless your beliefs are about having perfect health, they are not helping you.

The good news is that it is relatively easy to reprogram the subconscious mind through the repetition of thought. It's really no different than reprogramming a computer. The subconscious mind does not have the ability to reason, and so it accepts whatever you put into it. Like Genie in *Aladdin* the subconscious mind is at your every command.

Everything you're about to learn in this book is aimed toward reprogramming your subconscious mind to manifest health in your body, no matter what your circumstances are now. The following words and concepts are designed to expose and eradicate any negative beliefs you might have around illness, and the practices will help cement new beliefs about pure health into your subconscious mind. This is The Secret to Health.

Lesson 1

The Secret to Health Revealed

What does it mean to be healthy? You may think that being healthy means that you are not sick, but being healthy is far more than that. If you feel okay, or average, or nothing much at all, you are not healthy.

Being healthy is feeling the same way as little children feel. Little children are bursting with energy every day. Their bodies feel light and flexible; moving is effortless. They're light on their feet. Their minds are clear; they're happy, and free of worry and stress. They sleep deeply and peacefully every night, and they wake up feeling completely refreshed, as if with a brand-new body. They feel passionate and excited about every new day. Look at little children and you will see what being healthy really means. It is the way you used to feel, and it is the way you should *still* feel!

You can feel this way most of the time, because health is available to you unceasingly. There is never a second that anything is withheld from you. Whatever you want is yours, and that includes health. But you have to open the door to receive it!

When you know The Secret, you will understand that you can have *anything* you choose: true happiness, wonderful relationships, abundant wealth, and certainly great health. If you think about it, health is the most precious thing in life, and yet more than anything else, we can take our health for granted. For many of us, the only time we think of our health is when we lose it. Then the realization hits us: without our health, we have nothing.

But with the knowledge of The Secret, you can enjoy the greatest health and vitality every day, and for the rest of your life. You can also recover from any health crisis, heal any injury, or cure yourself of any disease.

I know of miracles that have taken place in health where there seemed to be no hope: failed kidneys regenerated, diseased hearts healed, eyesight restored, tumors disappeared, and bones grown and rebuilt by themselves. I've had people write to me describing how they cured themselves of diabetes, tuberculosis, multiple sclerosis, epilepsy, and various forms of cancer. I know of people who were in depression and were catapulted into joyful and fulfilling lives. I know people who have suffered from anxiety and every kind of mental illness who have restored themselves to perfect mental health.

And all of this happened because of knowing how to apply The Secret.

What Is The Secret?

The Secret is one of the most powerful laws in the Universe—the law of attraction.

The law of attraction responds to and materializes your dominant thoughts. Whatever you think about and focus on will appear in your life. It doesn't matter who you are or where you are, the law of attraction is forming your entire life experience, and this all-powerful law is doing that through your thoughts. You are the one who calls the law of attraction into action, and you do it through your thoughts.

How exactly does it work?

It has long been known that matter, or physical objects, are really just packets of energy at a microscopic level. Well, cutting edge science has confirmed that every thought is made up of energy too, and has its own unique frequency. And when the energy and frequency of a single thought radiate out into the Universe, they affect those things in the material world that are of the same frequency. According to the law of attraction, "like attracts like." That means your thoughts magnetically attract to themselves anything that is on a "like," or similar, frequency. As a single thought radiates out, it is magnetically attracted to the energy and frequencies of similar thoughts, similar objects, and even similar people, and draws those things back to you. In other words, your thoughts attract the very things you are thinking about, and so, through this most powerful law, your thoughts become the things in your life. Your thoughts become things! Say this over to yourself and let it seep into your consciousness:

Your thoughts become things!

The law of attraction responds to your thoughts, no matter what they may be. If you can think about what you want, and make those your dominant thoughts, you *will* bring what you want into your life. This is particularly true when it comes to your health, as a single thought, repeated over and over, becomes entrenched as a belief in the subconscious mind. Remember, the health of the body is entirely governed by the subconscious mind.

The repercussions of this from a health perspective are nothing short of phenomenal. As you think of yourself living in perfect health, you are powerfully and consciously determining your future health and well-being—your thoughts are directing your subconscious to command perfect health through the law of attraction. It's that easy.

So why isn't everybody living in perfect health? It's because the law of attraction is giving them what they are thinking about—period!

The Law of Attraction Is Impersonal

The law of attraction is a law of nature. It is impersonal and therefore responds to all thoughts in the same way, whether positive or negative. The law of attraction does not favor health over disease, it simply gives you whatever it is you are thinking about. The law of attraction is permanently receiving your thoughts and reflecting them back to you as the people, circumstances, and events in your life experience.

The primary reason why people do not have the health they want is because they are thinking more about what they *don't* want than what they *do* want. They think more about disease than they do about health and well-being.

If a patient is focused on illness, then they are inadvertently bringing more illness to them through the law of attraction. On the other hand, if the patient focuses on health and removes all notion of illness from their thoughts and feelings, then through the law of attraction they must produce health.

I have two friends who both coincidentally contracted the virus that causes the shingles rash around the same time. They were each told that shingles is treatable with antibiotics, but that it can take anywhere from a week to two months to cure. They were also warned that it could be quite painful and debilitating. So we have two people: same age, same symptoms, same diagnosis. The

difference was that one of them chose to think
hopeful, grateful, and appreciative thoughts:
firstly about the antibiotics, and secondly for his
own health and his body's ability to heal itself.
He recovered from the shingles in just a few days,
with no painful side effects. The second person
had the opposite response. He had a lot of anxious
and fearful thoughts, not just for the pain he fully
expected, but for the days of work he would lose
and how that would impact his business. He came
to resent the disease. Sure enough, he was struck
down for almost eight weeks, and he continues to
fear a relapse.

Keep in mind that anytime you are listening to
someone talk about their illness, and you focus on
that illness, you are inviting illness to you. Instead,
think thoughts of health, speak words of health,
and give thanks for your health and well-being.

The "Don't Want" Epidemic

An epidemic worse than any plague that
humankind has ever seen has been raging
for centuries. It is the "don't want" epidemic.
People keep this epidemic alive when they
predominantly think, speak, act, and focus on
what they "don't want."

When you focus your thoughts on something you want, or on something you *don't* want, and you hold that focus, you are in that moment summoning that thing to you with the mightiest power in the Universe. The law of attraction doesn't compute "don't" or "not" or "no," or any other words of negation. As you speak words of negation, the law of attraction is receiving the opposite message:

So if you say, "I don't want to catch the flu."

The law of attraction receives, *"I want to catch the flu."*

When you say, "I don't want a headache."

The law of attraction hears, *"I want a headache."*

When you say, "I don't want to fall and hurt myself."

The law of attraction hears, *"I want to fall and hurt myself."*

When you say, "I don't want to gain weight."

The law of attraction hears, *"I want to gain weight."*

When you say, "I don't want to make myself sick."

The law of attraction hears, *"I want to make myself sick."*

You attract to you what you think about most, and that's why all of this "don't want" talk is really responsible for what has become a "don't want" epidemic! The majority of the population are inadvertently filling all aspects of their lives with what they don't want, and they can't understand why life is not improving.

The current state of your body and your current level of health are really just a reflection of your past thoughts. It is easy to see what your dominant thoughts have been regarding your health, because that is what you have experienced. This remains true regardless of whether these dominant thoughts are of things you want, or whether they are part of the "don't want" epidemic.

It also remains true for people dealing with chronic disease or long-term health conditions. Many people instinctively attempt to fight the disease in order to overcome it. But according to the law of attraction, the path to eradicating disease is not to fight it.

What You Resist Persists

The renowned Swiss psychologist Carl Jung said: "What you resist persists." When we're fighting something, we're resisting it.

The reason that what you resist persists is because if you're resisting something it means you passionately *don't* want it, which translates as *want it* to the law of attraction, and therefore you are inviting it to you. In fact, the more you *don't want* the disease you're experiencing, the more you increase it. As you resist the disease, you are adding more feelings, more energy, and more power to the disease, and you are bringing more of it at a furious rate. It can only get bigger, because that is the law.

At thirty years of age, one woman decided that she would attempt to cure herself of epilepsy, a neurological disease that had afflicted her since she was a child. She knew that epilepsy in the form that she suffered was considered by most neurologists to be incurable. Doctors in these cases tend to prescribe strong medication simply to numb the mind and sedate misfiring neurons to ward off the worst seizures. After decades of feeling that the disease and the medication owned her, this woman decided to try a different approach. If successful, it would allow her to regain focus and sharpness of mind, and be free of all neurological symptoms. She was determined to do everything she could to heal her brain and nervous system. She knew that her epileptic seizures were triggered by stress and anxiety, so the first thing she did was to simplify her life. She took the time to relax and to focus on feeling good. She did this through healthy living, love, and showing gratitude and patience, both to herself and others. She refused to entertain any negative thoughts about her nervous system or her brain. She also read up on neuroplasticity, a new science that reveals the brain's ability to change, rewire, and to heal itself. And so, with all the faith that she could muster, she believed that her neurons, her brain, and her entire nervous system could be remade. Remarkably, within days of beginning, she felt as though she had a whole new body. And one year later, she is free of all neurological symptoms. She no longer needs to take the mind-numbing medications, and she is sharper and more focused than she has been for her whole life.

This woman chose to live according to the law of attraction. She did not own the prognosis of epilepsy in her mind, nor did she attempt to fight the condition. Instead, she focused on a healthy brain, and she owned a healthy brain as a result.

Let's all be grateful for our healthy brains!

You Create Your Life

You create your whole life, including the health of your body and mind, through your thoughts and the law of attraction. It doesn't just work if you know about it. It has always been working in your life and every other person's life throughout history. When you become aware of this great law, then you become *aware* of how incredibly powerful you are, to be able to change your life and *think* a new life into existence.

Whether you realize it or not, you are thinking most of the time. What you think about the most or focus on the most is what will appear in your life. Whatever you sow, you reap! Your thoughts are seeds, and the harvest you reap will depend on the seeds you plant.

If you are complaining about your lack of health, the law of attraction will powerfully bring more situations of a lack of health for you to complain about. If you are listening to someone else complain about an illness and you are focusing on that, sympathizing with them, agreeing with them, in that moment you are attracting illness to yourself.

Whatever thoughts you focus on will materialize and come into your life. The law is simply reflecting and giving back to you exactly what you are focusing on with your thoughts. "Focusing on perfect health" is something we can all do within ourselves, despite what may be happening on the outside.

With this powerful knowledge, you can completely change every circumstance to do with your health by changing the way you think.

Your health is in your hands. No matter where you are now, no matter what has happened in your life, you can begin to *consciously* choose your thoughts, and you can change your life. There is no such thing as a hopeless situation, just as there is no such thing as an incurable disease; at some point in time, every so-called incurable disease has been cured. In my mind, and in the world I create, "incurable" does not exist. There is plenty of room for you in this world, so come join me and all who are here. It is the world where "miracles" are everyday occurrences. It is a world overflowing with a total abundance of good health and well-being, where *all* good things exist now, within you. Sounds like heaven, doesn't it? It is.

Lesson 2

Health and the Subconscious Mind

It has been said that "natural forces within us are the true healers of disease."

If there was no healing power within us, nothing could be healed.

From ancient spiritual traditions we are told that the health of the body is governed entirely by the subconscious mind. That's to say, all functions of the body, from the respiratory system to digestion, to the central nervous system and the immune system, are under the watchful eye of the subconscious mind. You don't think about breathing or digesting or pumping blood . . . those functions happen automatically, regulated by your subconscious mind. Likewise, if you cut your finger, you don't have to wonder how to stem the bleeding. Your subconscious mind steps up and orders the body to do what it was designed to do. It heals itself. It works in every system, on every level, throughout your entire body; whatever your subconscious mind orders, your body delivers. It's a perfect reflection of the law of attraction in action. Just as in the outer world where your thoughts attract the people, circumstances, and events to deliver whatever it is you are thinking about, so too in the inner world of your body. Your subconscious mind attracts the circumstances and events that make up the health of your body.

To fully realize and appreciate the power your subconscious mind has over your body, you need to know about the incredible world inside your body—because all of it is under your command!

Your Incredible Body

All the cells in your body have a role to play, and they work together for the sole purpose of giving you life. Some cells are the leaders of particular regions or organs, and they manage and direct all the working cells in their region, like your heart, brain, liver, kidneys, or lungs. However, these leader cells work under a hierarchy, reporting directly to their superior, the subconscious mind. The leader cells of any organ direct and manage all the other cells working in that organ, ensuring order and harmony so the organ works perfectly. Patrol cells travel throughout the sixty thousand miles of blood vessels in your body to maintain order and peace. When there is a disturbance, such as a scratch to the skin, the patrol cells immediately signal the alert, and the subconscious mind orders the appropriate repair team to rush to the area. In the case of a scratch, for example, the first on the scene is the blood-clotting team, and they work to arrest the blood flow. After their work is done, the tissue and skin teams move in to do the repair work to the area, mending the tissue, and sealing the skin.

If an intruder enters your body, like a bacterial infection or virus, the subconscious mind immediately takes an imprint of the intruder. The imprint is checked against records to see if there is a match with previous intruders. If a match is found, the subconscious mind immediately notifies the relevant attack team to destroy the intruder. If there is no match, the subconscious mind opens up a new file on the intruder, and *all* the attack teams are summoned to move in and destroy the intruder. Whichever attack team is successful in destroying the intruder is then recorded by the subconscious mind. If the intruder returns, the subconscious mind will know who it is dealing with and exactly how to deal with it.

If for any reason a cell of your body begins to change its behavior and cease to work for the good of the body, the patrol cells signal the subconscious mind, which then orders the rescue team to rush in to repair or eliminate the cell. If a cell needs a particular chemical to be repaired, it is found inside your natural pharmacy. You have a complete pharmacy operating inside you that can produce every healing chemical that a pharmaceutical company can produce.

All cells must work as a team, twenty-four hours a day, seven days a week, for their entire life. Their sole purpose is to maintain the life and health in your body. You have around 100 trillion cells in your body working nonstop to give you life! All 100 trillion cells are under your command via your subconscious mind.

How you *consciously* command your subconscious mind and the cells of your body requires a little more understanding of just how your subconscious mind works. Your subconscious mind is like a computer; it has many different programs that you have loaded into it. You do this through your thoughts and beliefs, or by listening to and accepting other people's thoughts and beliefs. And you've been doing this throughout your life. All the programs in your subconscious mind have been put there by you, and it's through forming new thoughts and beliefs that you can create a new program and override the old one.

To know what programs you have placed in your subconscious mind regarding your health, you must consider the *conscious* thoughts and beliefs you hold about your body and your health— because whatever you believe, your subconscious mind believes too.

Check Your Beliefs

Perhaps you have come to believe something like "I catch colds easily," "I have a sensitive stomach," "I find it hard to lose weight," "I'm allergic to that," or "It runs in our family." All these are beliefs, not facts, and they are beliefs that do not serve you. Whatever you believe and feel is true *will* be true for you, whether those beliefs help you or harm you.

Clearly, it's imperative that you start thinking about things that serve your health rather than harm your health. The more you do that, the sooner these positive thoughts will form your new beliefs around health. All beliefs are simply repeated thoughts with strong feelings attached to them.

Whatever you believe about your body on a conscious level, your subconscious mind believes too because it lacks the faculty of reason. As a consequence, your subconscious mind passes on all of your *conscious* thoughts and beliefs as a direct order to your cells. Your subconscious mind doesn't question anything you believe. In fact, it has received every thought and every belief you've ever had.

The way your subconscious mind works and the way your cells respond to your every thought or belief is simply the law of attraction working inside your body. If you think or say, "I always get jet lag when I travel," your subconscious mind sends "jet lag" as a command to the cells, and they must carry out your instructions and produce the symptoms of "jet lag." Believe you have a weight problem, your subconscious mind orders the cells in your body to respond with a weight problem. The subconscious mind must follow your instructions and keep your body in an overweight condition until you change your belief. Be afraid you might catch an illness, the cells receive the message of illness from the subconscious mind, and they immediately get busy creating the symptoms of the illness. And of course, the opposite is also true. When you believe you can restore health to your body, your subconscious mind believes it too, and consequently orders your cells to get to work restoring health.

A woman who is very near and dear to me had suffered from various allergies for most of her life. The worst of these was her reaction to heat, which began as an itching sense in her hands that later spread to her feet and other parts of her body. She had come to believe that it was a form of eczema, but a friend suggested it might be something more serious, and that she should get it checked out. After extensive testing, her doctor informed her that she was suffering from an autoimmune disease of the liver with no known cure. Basically, her immune system was attacking perfectly healthy cells and tissue under the mistaken belief that they were diseased. This was causing a buildup of toxins in her liver, a situation that can eventually lead to liver failure and the need for a transplant.

Being very familiar with the law of attraction, she knew that her thoughts and beliefs were the ultimate cause of everything relating to her health, and that her immune system was simply acting out the beliefs of her subconscious mind. To restore her health, she needed to change her beliefs, consciously and subconsciously, all the way down to the cellular level. However, she was concerned that she couldn't simply flip the switch and know that she was healthy—that didn't seem believable to her. Instead, she felt she had to give her body and her subconscious mind something that they could genuinely believe would lead to health.

What she decided on was a drastic change of diet. She cut out all processed food and commenced an intensive program of juicing, using nothing but fresh, organic fruit and vegetables. She supplemented this with a nutritional multivitamin regimen. Her specialist was a little skeptical, as he advised her that there was no known connection between diet or vitamins and this particular disease. In truth, he was expecting to have to place her on the organ transplant list within months. But she stuck to her plan and maintained her strict juicing and multivitamin program.

At her very next checkup a few weeks later, her liver function blood work results showed a dramatic improvement. Subsequent tests over the next few months continued that remarkable trend. Her specialist was constantly amazed by the turnaround, and as he said to her, "Whatever it is you're doing, keep doing it!"

Of course, what she did was to change her beliefs—the juicing diet acted like a placebo to give her something to ground her new beliefs in. By changing her thoughts and changing her beliefs, she was able to take command of her subconscious mind as well as her immune system to overcome an "incurable" disease and create health in her body.

Let's be grateful for our perfectly healthy liver!

The Placebo Effect

You may have heard of the placebo effect in medicine, which is a perfect example of the power of the subconscious mind over healing. Whenever a pharmaceutical company wishes to prove the effectiveness of their latest drug, they recruit volunteer patients and divide them into two groups. One group of patients is given real pills or treatment, and another group is given the placebo—a sugar pill or fake treatment—but neither is told whether or not they're getting the

real medication that might cure them. To the great
frustration of the pharmaceutical company, the
group that gets the placebo often experiences
significant improvement and the reduction or
disappearance of symptoms. When patients *think*
and truly *believe* the sugar pill is a cure, their
subconscious mind commands the cells of the
body to cure all symptoms of the disease.

The startling results of the placebo effect regularly
demonstrate the power of beliefs on our body.

Your cells are your most loyal subjects who serve
you without question, and so whatever you think,
and whatever you believe, becomes the law of
your body. When you believe and think that aging
and deterioration or sickness are inevitable, then
they must happen.

On the other hand, if you want to feel as good as
you did when you were a child, then give your
cells these commands: "I feel amazing today," "I
have so much energy," "I have perfect eyesight,"
"I can eat whatever I want and maintain my ideal
weight," "I sleep like a baby every night," "I feel
as good as I did when I was a kid." Yes, you can
choose to *feel* young and to stop feeling your age.
Feeling your age is just a belief you've been given
and a program you've given to your body. You can

change the command you're giving whenever you want by changing what you believe!

A Brand-New Body

If you need further convincing that beliefs about aging are all in our minds, consider that science explains we have a brand-new body in a very short time. We create millions of new cells every second and cast off old ones. Parts of our body are replaced every day, other parts take a few months, and others a few years. But if our entire bodies are replaced within a few years, as science has proven, then how can it be that degeneration or aging occurs? It can only occur by thought, by observation of aging, and by the attention given to aging. Release those aging thoughts from your consciousness as best you can and know that your body is only months old, no matter how many birthdays you have chalked up in your mind.

I'd like to tell you how I overcame negative beliefs about aging, and used The Secret to heal my eyesight.

I had been wearing reading glasses for about three years before I discovered The Secret. One night as I was tracing the knowledge of The Secret back through the centuries, I found myself reaching for my glasses to see what I was reading. And I stopped in my tracks. The realization of what I had done struck me like a lightning bolt.

I had listened to society's message that eyesight diminishes with age. I had watched people stretch their arms out so that they could read something. I had given my thought to eyesight diminishing with age, and I had brought the reality to me. I hadn't done it deliberately, but I had done it. I knew that what I had brought into being with thoughts I could change, so I immediately imagined myself seeing as clearly as when I was twenty-one years old. I saw myself in dark restaurants, on planes, and at my computer, reading clearly and effortlessly. And I said over and over, "I can see clearly, I can see clearly." I felt the feelings of gratitude and excitement for having clear vision. In three days my eyesight had been restored, and I now do not own reading glasses. *I can see clearly.*

I didn't notice the three days that it took because I *knew* it was done in the moment I made the choice. If I had noticed the three days that it took, then I would have been noticing that it was not already done. I totally believed and *knew* it was done. I had absolute faith. I can just as easily say that it took me three days to realize that my eyes were seeing clearly or that it took me three days to adjust to my clear eyes. That would be true, because I knew the moment I made the choice that it had been given to me, and I had absolutely no doubt whatsoever. From that state of knowing, my eyesight became clear in three days.

When I told Dr. Ben Johnson, one of the teachers from *The Secret*, about what I had done, he said to me, "Do you realize what had to happen to your eyes for you to do that in three days?" I replied, "No, and thank goodness I didn't know, so that thought was not in my head! I just knew I could do it, and that I could do it fast." Sometimes less information is better! The restoration of my eyesight seemed like nothing to me. In fact, I expected my eyesight to come back overnight, so three days was no miracle in my mind.

By using your subconscious mind to instill new beliefs, you have the power to create health and happiness at levels far beyond what you might have experienced before. You can and should be full of vitality and joy, with an incredible zest for life. I am telling you this so that you can start to break the boundaries of your imagination and stop putting limits on your health, your happiness, and your life.

LESSON 3

FEEL GOOD—THE FAST TRACK TO GOOD HEALTH

Nothing can come into your experience unless you summon it through persistent thoughts. It is your persistent and dominant thoughts that engage the law of attraction so that you literally think your whole life into existence.

Your life is a reflection of what you hold inside you, and what you hold inside you is always under your control. There is no outside force that can affect your life, or indeed your health, unless you give something power through your thoughts and beliefs. The greatest power is within you—in what you think and what you believe.

With that in mind, you have a choice right now. Do you want to believe that your health is just the luck of the draw and bad things can happen to you at any time? Do you want to believe that you have no control over circumstances or what happens to your own body? That your health is simply a matter of luck?

Or do you want to believe and *know* that your health and well-being are in your hands and that only *good health* can come into your life, because that is the way you think and believe? You have a choice, and whatever you choose to think and whatever you believe *will* become your life experience.

No one would ever deliberately attract disease, chronic illness, or serious injury to themselves, but without the knowledge of The Secret, it is easy to see how some unwanted health conditions may have occurred in your life or other people's lives. They simply came from a lack of awareness of the great power of your thoughts and your subconscious mind. And as you now know, whatever you believe about your health is what your subconscious mind will bring to fruition, because your subconscious mind governs every aspect of your body and your health.

It is your thoughts that determine what your subconscious mind believes, and so it is clear— your thoughts are the primary cause of *everything*.

That being the case, it stands to reason that you might want to control what you're thinking about your health.

But with around sixty thousand thoughts in a day, how is it possible to control every single thought that pops into your head?

You can't do it, no matter how hard you try.

However, the good news is, it's actually your *dominant* thoughts that create new beliefs in the subconscious. It's your *dominant* thoughts that attract the people, circumstances, and events in your life; and it's your *dominant* thoughts that are literally thinking your life into existence.

Your dominant thoughts are the ones that you give the most attention to, and they are the thoughts you feel most strongly about. If you have a thought, and there is no feeling attached to that thought, it won't have the necessary power to attract anything. You see, your feelings add power to all your thoughts and words.

If at any time you want to know whether you've been thinking good thoughts or bad thoughts, you can just check in on how you're feeling. What you're feeling will tell you exactly what you've been thinking. If you feel good, you've been thinking good thoughts. If you feel bad, you've been thinking negative or bad thoughts. It is impossible to feel bad and at the same time be having good thoughts. That would defy the law, because your thoughts cause your feelings. If you are feeling bad, it is because you are thinking thoughts that are making you feel bad. Likewise, it is impossible to feel good and at the same time be having negative thoughts. If you are feeling good, it is because you are thinking good thoughts. You see, you can have whatever you want in your life, no limits. But there's one catch: you have to feel good.

And what you'll soon discover is: the better you feel, the better life gets.

The worse you feel, the worse life gets—until you change how you feel.

Your thoughts continue to be the primary source of everything, but your feelings are what gives booster power to those thoughts.

To Improve Anything, Change How You Feel

If you want your health to improve, you have to start having good thoughts and *feeling* good—now.

So what are you feeling now? Take a few moments to think about how you feel.

If you are feeling good, then great! Keep doing whatever you are doing and you can rest assured that your thoughts are good, and you are attracting all good things—including good health.

If you are not feeling so good, then you need to change whatever you are thinking until you *do* feel good. Your health depends on it.

Of course, it can be quite challenging for someone to suddenly change the way they feel, especially if they happen to be physically unwell, in pain, or if they've just received a troubling diagnosis. It's nearly impossible to leap from pain or despair to joyful happiness with the flick of a switch. But what you can do is *gradually* change your feelings by changing the way you are thinking. Take your mind and your attention away from whatever is making you feel bad. Put off any thoughts about sickness or disease, and focus on things that actually make you feel good, things that can change your feelings in a snap. They might be beautiful memories, future events, funny moments, nature, a person you love, your favorite music. Different things will affect you at different times, so if one doesn't work, go to another. It only takes a minute or two of changing focus to something good to begin to change the way you feel.

A young woman had just broken up with her boyfriend and was out of work, away from family in a distant city, and at the lowest phase of her life, when she was diagnosed with acute tuberculosis. Her doctor gave her a grim prognosis, suggesting that she had no more than a 10 percent chance of recovery. She felt completely broken and devoid of hope. But something within her refused to give in to the disease or give up on life. Despite her circumstances, she committed herself to engaging in all the little things that made her feel good: talking to friends, listening to her favorite music, walking in nature, and watching the sunset. Anything that made her happy. She became more and more optimistic with each passing day. At her next appointment, her doctor was shocked by her recovery. Tears of happiness flowed as she realized she had overcome tuberculosis simply by feeling good.

What this woman did was to elevate herself to the frequency of feeling good, where all circumstances and events surrounding good health are residing. Good thoughts, good feelings, good health.

Let's all feel good about fresh air and healthy lungs!

When you have good feelings, or when you feel love for anything—for a sunny day, for your home, a friend, or your dog—your body receives the full force of natural health at an astounding rate. When you feel bad about yourself or anything else, the tension causes your nerves and cells to contract; the vital chemical production in your body changes, your blood vessels contract, and your breathing becomes shallow—each of which reduces the force of health in your organs and your entire body. It doesn't matter if you feel bad about a subject that has nothing to do with your health; when you feel bad, you reduce the force of natural health to your body.

Laughter Is the Best Medicine

You will have heard the common saying that laughter is the best medicine.

Well, it's certainly true that one of the fastest and best ways to relieve tension and dissolve disease in our bodies is through the power of laughter and joy.

One person who was inspired to include laughter as part of his healing was a man by the name of Norman Cousins. Norman had been diagnosed with an "incurable" disease. The doctors told him he had just a few months to live. Norman decided to heal himself. For three months all he did was watch comedy movies and laugh as much as possible. The disease left his body in those three months, and the doctors proclaimed his recovery a miracle. As he laughed, Norman released all negativity, and he released the disease.

Laughter releases negativity, and leads to miraculous cures. Laughter really is the best medicine.

Conversely, as nineteenth-century author Prentice Mulford once said: *"Let us remember, so far as we can, that every unpleasant thought is a bad thing literally put in the body."*

Science has shown that negative thoughts and stress can seriously degrade the body and the brain's functioning. On the other hand, happier thoughts remove physiological stress from the body, which allows the body to do exactly what it was designed to do—heal itself.

Start thinking happy thoughts and start *being* happy. You have your finger on the *"being* happy" button. Press it now and keep your finger pressed down on it firmly, no matter what is happening around you.

If you make a decision that from here onward you will give the majority of your attention to happy thoughts, you will begin a process of purifying your body. Those happy thoughts will supply your body with the greatest health booster you could possibly give it.

There are endless excuses not to be happy. But if you put happiness off by saying, "I'll be happy when . . . ," you'll not only be delaying happiness for the rest of your life, you'll also be diminishing the health of your body. Happiness is your body's miracle health elixir, so be happy now, no excuses!

> *A young mother wrote to TheSecret.tv to tell of her journey with cancer at the young age of twenty-seven. She'd been given a bleak prognosis, and her focus was simply survival. Then, on a visit to her oncologist, she bumped into a friend of her grandparents', who offered the most priceless*

advice that anyone could receive in that situation. She was told to only allow happiness into her life, to laugh as much as possible, and to distance herself from any negative situations or people. From that moment on, she only welcomed happy people and happy emotions, and she watched only happy movies. In this way, she made sure that each step she took was a happy step in the right direction, and that every single day would be better than the day before.

Six months later, she was told that her treatment had been successful and the tumor was completely gone. She attributes this to two things: the advice of her guardian angel in the oncologist's waiting room, and her ability to love her way back to health through unbridled happiness and feeling good.

Let's all take a moment to feel good!

Every moment you feel good, you are actively eliminating any negativity in your body! If you find it difficult to feel good about your health, all that matters is that you feel good about something, so surround yourself with everything you love, and use those things to feel as good as you can. Use everything you can in the outside world so that you feel good. Watch movies that make you laugh and feel good, not movies that make you feel tense or sad. Listen to music that makes you feel good. Get people to tell you jokes that make you laugh, or have them tell you funny stories about their most embarrassing moments. You know the things you love. You know your favorite things. You know what makes you happy, so draw on them all and feel as good as you can.

It's also very important to feel good when you're having any kind of medical test. Whether it's having your eyesight tested or blood pressure checked, getting an annual physical, or any examination concerning your health, it is important that you are feeling good during the appointment. And likewise, make sure you feel really good while receiving the results, in order to receive the best outcome. By the law of attraction, the results of any test must match the frequency you're on, so to bring the good outcome you want, you must be on the frequency to receive it!

A young wife and mother did all that and much more when she discovered an ominous-looking mole on her leg. After consulting a dermatologist, it was agreed to remove the mole and send it for biopsy. Then came a stressful weeklong wait for the results. During that time, the woman made every effort to resist indulging any negative thoughts and feelings about her health. But most important of all, she imagined what would happen when the hospital called with the results. She role-played the entire conversation in her mind in detail and felt the feelings of joy and relief for the good news that she was receiving. She endeavored to get on that feeling frequency of joy and relief as often as possible right up until the call came in. On the seventh day, the hospital called with the biopsy results — the mole was benign, exactly the result she had hoped for.

Let's all be grateful now for beautiful, healthy skin!

The outcome of every situation in your life will always match your frequency because that is how the law of attraction works! To get yourself onto a good feeling frequency about a test, imagine the outcome you want and feel that you have already received that outcome. Keep doing the practice until you feel good when you think about the test. Every possible outcome can happen, but you must be on a good feeling frequency to receive good outcomes.

Your Perfect Weight

The same principles work—by law—for any change you want in your body, including weight loss. If you want to lose weight, first feel good, feel the feelings of your perfect weight, and you will summon it to you. Don't focus on "losing weight." Instead, focus on your perfect weight. Many people who diet lose the weight and then put it back on, because their focus was on losing weight. If your focus is on losing weight then you must attract back the circumstances of needing to lose weight. Instead, make your perfect weight your focus. Whatever is your strongest focus is what you will attract. That is how the law works.

The most important thing—more than anything else—is to be in joy and to be happy *now*, despite your weight. If you can be in joy now, to the point where you feel so good that the weight doesn't matter so much anymore, then it will fall away. But first, you must feel good. You must feel good about you. This is so important, because you cannot attract your perfect weight if you feel bad about your body now. Feeling bad about your body is a powerful feeling, and you will continue to attract feeling bad about your body. You will never change your body if you are critical of it and find fault with it, and in fact you will attract more weight to you. Praise and bless every square inch of your body. Think about all the perfect things about you. As you think perfect thoughts, as you feel good about you, you are on the frequency of your perfect weight, and you are summoning perfection.

A teenage girl had been uncomfortable with her body since she was quite young. She had always been unusually tall for her age, and she would often go home crying to her parents because she was not the same as all the other girls. As she grew, her poor self-image led to her putting on weight, which then led to her feeling guilty whenever she ate. She tried hard to lose weight, and even though she was very diligent with dieting and working out, she never got the result she was looking for.

It all turned around for her once she learned to love her own body. In fact, she came to adore her body, she began to love her food, and miraculously the weight just fell away. She finally achieved her ideal weight. She was grateful for her height and in love with her body—she believed and knew she was perfect.

Let's give thanks for our perfect body and our perfect weight!

You really can *think and feel* your way to the perfect state of health, the perfect body, and the perfect weight. You can bring it into being through your positive thoughts and through feeling good about you. Good health is your birthright! You are the creator of you, and the law of attraction is your magnificent tool to create the perfect version of you.

LESSON 4

THE CREATIVE PROCESS FOR HEALTH

Whether it's bringing something you want, like a fitter, slimmer body, or changing something you don't want, like an illness or disease, the Creative Process is an easy guideline for you to create what you want for your health in three simple steps.

Ask. Believe. Receive.

Step 1: ASK

Ask yourself, what do you really want?

Remember the story of Genie, who emerges from the lamp to grant Aladdin's every wish? Well, you have your own Genie, and it's called the law of attraction. It listens to your every thought, your every wish, your every desire. And it makes all your dreams come true. All you have to do is ask.

When it comes to your health, just like everything else, you get to choose what you want, but you must get clear about it. This is your work. If you're not clear, then the law of attraction cannot bring you what you want. You will be sending out a mixed frequency and you can only attract mixed results. Perhaps for the first time in your life, work out what it is you really want for your health and your body, no limitations.

Do you want to cure a disease? Do you want to lose weight? Do you want to fully heal a painful injury? Would you like to look younger?

Now that you know you can have, be, or do anything, and there are no limits, what do you *really* want?

> *A firefighter was badly injured on duty, fracturing his tibia and breaking a bone in his ankle in half. He awoke from emergency surgery with bone grafts and rods in his leg holding his ankle together. He couldn't even feel his foot due to nerve damage.*

*The surgeon informed him that due to the severity
of the injury, he was still facing a 90 percent
chance of suffering permanent damage to his ankle
and a complete loss of mobility. But this firefighter
was determined to beat those odds. Throughout his
challenging recuperation, he remained positive,
writing in his journal exactly what he wanted. He
wanted to be healed, he wanted to walk and run
again, and he wanted to be an active father to his
young children. It took a full year of rehab, during
which time he literally had to learn to walk again.
But his doctor was shocked by the extent to which
this man was able to heal. From the outset he asked
for a full recovery, and that's exactly what he
achieved.*

Let's be grateful for our strong and healthy bones!

Most people think to ask for health only when
they don't have it, but you can ask for great
health at any time. Use the power of your
intention every single day and ask to be totally
healthy and well.

Step 2: BELIEVE

You must believe that you have received the
health that you are asking for. You must know

that a healthy body, the perfect weight, or looking younger is yours the moment you ask. You must have complete and utter faith.

Remember that when you believe something on a conscious level, that belief passes through unfiltered to the subconscious mind, which regulates and governs all aspects of your health and the 100 trillion cells in your body.

In the moment you ask and then *believe* you already have perfect health, all the cells of your body and in fact the entire Universe shift to bring it into existence. You must act, speak, and think as though you are receiving perfect health *now*. Why? Because for the law of attraction there is no time. There is no past or future. The law of attraction only operates on this present moment now. So if you want perfect health, see yourself as being in perfect health in this moment. If your thoughts contain noticing you do not have it yet, you will continue to attract not having it yet. You must believe you have it already. You must believe you have received it. You have to emit the belief of having received it now, in order to materialize it into your life. You have to believe it so deeply that your subconscious accepts it as true. When you do that, the law of attraction will powerfully move all circumstances, people, and events for you to receive.

Many people have more fearful beliefs about disease than they have good beliefs about health. It's not surprising because of the attention that is given to disease in the world, and you are surrounded by that every day. In spite of all the advances in medicine, disease is increasing, in part because people have become increasingly focused on and fearful of disease.

Do you believe in the inevitability of disease more than you believe in lifelong health? If you believe that your body will deteriorate with age and that disease is inevitable, your subconscious mind believes it too, and through the law of attraction it must reflect that back as the circumstances and state of your health and body.

If you've developed negative beliefs about your health, go back to the negotiating table. It's never too late to change your mind, which is essential if you want to change your health. Being healthy means having a healthy body *and* a healthy mind. You can't be happy or healthy if your mind is full of negative thoughts or negative beliefs. If you can keep your mind healthy, you will help the health of your body. One way to keep your mind healthy is to simply choose not to believe negative thoughts. When we don't give any attention to negative thoughts, they are depleted of energy and will dissolve immediately. Instead, we can choose to feed our body with positive thoughts about health, which prevents negative thoughts from existing at the same time.

How do you get yourself to a point of believing perfect health is yours? Start make believing. Be like a child, and make believe. Play, pretend, and make up games that will infiltrate your subconscious with the feeling of good health and well-being. Think only of health. Speak only of health. Act as if you have your ideal state of health already. As you make believe, you will begin to *believe* you have received. The law of attraction is responding to your dominant thoughts all the time, not just in the moment you ask. That's why after you've asked, you must continue to *believe* and *know*. Your belief that you have something, that undying faith, is your greatest power. When you believe you are receiving, get ready, and watch the magic begin!

One woman used make-believe in order to overcome chronic pain. For several months, she had been suffering from a degenerative disk disease, which resulted in severe pain around her thoracic spine and ribs. She was surviving on pain-relief medication and spent much of her time lying down unable to move but also unable to sleep on account of the pain. With no other help available from modern medicine, she decided to take control of her own self-healing. She imagined her healing cells as an army of tiny critters called "Joy Bugs" who would patrol her bloodstream until they confronted the enemy—the pain and inflammation. They would then attack by "hugging" the diseased cells into submission. She thanked the universe for her healing and fell asleep. On the first night that she imagined this scenario, she slept soundly. She awoke, got herself ready, and was halfway down the stairs before realizing that she felt no pain for the first time in months. She was able to go the whole day without the need for pain medication. And that was just the first day of many pain-free days to come now that she truly believed in her own ability to self-heal.

Let's be grateful for our body's miraculous ability to heal itself!

How the Universe will bring perfect health to you is not your concern or job. When you are trying to work out *how* it will happen, you are emitting a frequency that contains a lack of belief—that you don't believe you have it already. You think *you* have to do it and you do not believe the Universe will do it *for* you. But the *how* is not your part in the Creative Process. Allow the Universe to take care of it.

Step 3: RECEIVE

Ask once, believe you have received, and all you have to do to receive is feel good. When you are feeling good, you are on the frequency of receiving. You are on the frequency of all good things coming to you, and you will receive what you have asked for. You wouldn't ask for anything unless it was going to make you feel good in the receiving of it, would you? So get yourself on the feel-good frequency, and you will receive.

A fast way to get yourself on that frequency is to say, "I am receiving now. I am receiving all the good in my life now. I am receiving the perfect state of health, the perfect body, the perfect weight, unlimited energy and vitality now." And *feel* it. *Feel* it now, as though you have already received it.

When you *feel* as though you have something now, and the feeling is so real that it is like you have it already, you are believing that you have received, and you will receive.

A young, single father was admitted to hospital with very high blood pressure after experiencing symptoms for over a month. He was diagnosed with congestive heart failure and was immediately transferred to intensive care, where he remained for six days. Further testing revealed that his heart had become enlarged and had grown thick muscle. All he kept hearing from doctors was what poor condition his heart was in and how his blood pressure was off the charts. This had him wondering whether or not he would even make it. But he knew enough to turn his predominant thoughts to hope, and to believe that his heart was strong and healthy and full of love. Most importantly, he felt a strong, healthy, normal heart beating inside his chest as though he'd already received it.

Several months after his stay in intensive care, he was scheduled for some follow-up tests, where diagnostic imaging revealed a perfectly healthy, normal heart. His doctor was astonished, as this level of recovery was most unusual. This young father put it down to his thoughts and beliefs. As he says, when the doctors spoke of heart failure, he chose to ask, believe, and receive heart success.

Let's all be grateful for our healthy hearts!

Manifesting Health for Others

Under certain circumstances, it's possible to use the creative process to help improve the health of others.

A dear friend of mine, Marcy, is one of the greatest manifestors I have seen. She *feels* everything. She *feels* what it would be like to have what she is asking for. She *feels* everything into existence. She *feels* good health and well-being, not just for herself but for all those she loves. When her husband became gravely ill, Marcy set about *feeling* what it would be like when her husband made a full recovery. She didn't get caught up in how, or when, she just *felt* it every single day until it manifested. Her husband made a full and miraculous recovery.

If you want to help someone you love who is ill, you can use the Creative Process to ask, believe, and to *feel* full health being restored to them. Of course, each one of us is the creator of our own life, and we cannot create in someone else's life unless the other person is consciously asking for that same thing. For example, when someone wants to be well, then others around that person can use their powerful focus on pure wellness for them. The positive energy will be received by the person because they are asking for it themselves, and it will help them enormously. So while you cannot override what another person is attracting through their own thoughts and feelings, if they are also asking for health for themselves your good thoughts and feelings can help them rise to a frequency where they can receive health.

Inspired Action

Often, when people are confronted by a health issue, they want to know what *action* steps they should take to remedy the situation. Follow the action steps of your preferred healthcare professional and subsequent treatment plan if that is what you've chosen. But in terms of the law of attraction there are no action steps required. Simply follow the three steps of the Creative Process: Ask, Believe, and Receive. However, you may choose to take some *inspired action* within the receiving step of the Creative Process.

It's important to note that *action* and *inspired action* are not the same thing. *Action* is a word that can imply "work" to some people, but *inspired action* will not feel like work at all. The difference between inspired action and action is this: inspired action is when you are acting to receive.

If you are in action to try to make it happen, you have slipped backward. Inspired action is effortless, and it feels wonderful because you are on the frequency of receiving.

When it comes to your health, always trust your instincts. It's the Universe inspiring you. It's the Universe communicating with you on the receiving frequency. If you have an intuitive or instinctive feeling to take a certain step or make a certain decision in regard to your health, follow it, and you will find that the Universe is magnetically moving you to receive what you asked for.

Whatever actions you take, make sure that they are consistent with what you asked for and do not contradict your desire. This is where the practice of "acting as if" can come into effect. Ask yourself, "What steps would I be taking right now if I already had what I want?"

I know of a couple who were desperately trying to conceive a child. Sadly, there were fertility challenges on both sides, and after a failed IVF attempt, they were down to their last few eggs. Even their fertility doctor felt discouraged about another attempt. Nevertheless, this couple was determined to try again. This time, however, they switched up their actions to match their desire. They stopped longing for a baby and began to act as if their baby was about to arrive. They opened up the room that they planned to use as a nursery and removed all the non-baby furniture and other items that they were storing in there, and they made space in the wardrobe and bought baby clothes. And sure enough, on the next IVF cycle, with one of the last available eggs, they became pregnant with what would be their beautiful baby daughter.

Let's give thanks for all the beautiful babies and children in the world!

In summary, the Creative Process is your first aid kit to help eliminate disease and attract perfect health. All it requires is that you follow these steps:

Step 1: Get clear on the state of health you want. Have a picture in your mind of what you will look like when you have achieved perfect health—free of any symptoms and able to do all the things you like to do. Get pictures of yourself in perfect health, if you have them, and look at them often.

Step 2: You must believe you will receive and that perfect health is yours already. You must imagine, pretend, act as if, and make believe that perfect health is yours. You must see yourself as having that perfect health you've asked for.

Do not contradict what you have asked for with your thoughts, words, and actions. Do not speak of any illness or symptoms, and do not hide away under a blanket wearing your pajamas all day and feeling sorry for yourself. Have faith and focus on all the things you will do with perfect health.

Make it your intention to look for, admire, and inwardly praise people who have your idea of perfect health. Seek them out, and as you admire them and feel the feelings of that—you are summoning it to you. If you see people who are unwell, immediately switch your mind to a picture of them and yourself in perfect health and *feel* it.

Step 3: All you need to do to get yourself on the frequency of receiving perfect health is feel good. It is vital that you feel good, because you will never attract perfect health while you are feeling miserable about your symptoms. If you feel bad about your health, you will not be on the right frequency to eradicate illness. Instead, you must feel joy, feel happiness, and think thoughts of perfect health until you are on the frequency of perfect health. And then that is exactly what you will receive.

Now you might understand why a person who says, and more importantly *believes*, "I stay healthy all winter," always seems to breeze through the winter months in perfect health. Or why a person who says, "I hate the springtime, I have a lot of allergies," always seems to be sneezing and have watery eyes and a bright red nose for at least three months of the year. These people *expect* wellness or sickness. If you can begin to expect nothing but *good* health, and make it a daily habit, you will be setting the universal forces ahead of you to summon perfect health.

LESSON 5

GRATITUDE FOR HEALTH

Are you grateful for your health when it's good? Or do you only notice your health when your body gets sick or hurts?

Are you grateful when you have a good night's sleep? Or do you take those nights for granted and only think of sleep when you've been deprived of it?

Are you grateful to be alive each day?

Health is a gift of life; it is something you receive and continue to receive, each day. In addition to everything else we do to be healthy, we have to be grateful for our health in order to continue to receive more health!

Gratitude is one of the fastest ways I know to begin experiencing the full state of health you are meant to have in your body and mind. If you use gratitude a little, your life and your health will change a little. If you use gratitude a lot, every day, your life and especially your health will change in ways you can hardly imagine now. Not only does gratitude multiply everything good in your life, it also eliminates the negative things, including illness and disease. No matter what negative situation you may find yourself in, you can *always* find something to be grateful for. And as you do, you harness the power of gratitude that eliminates all negativity in your life, no matter what form it has taken.

Gratitude Creates Miracles

Gratitude can create miracles, move mountains, and part seas. And gratitude can dissolve any disease.

If you don't believe gratitude has the power to create miracles in your health and body, then consider these incredible stories:

A young woman was diagnosed with alopecia, otherwise known as hair loss or baldness, when alarming clumps of hair began falling from her scalp. She tried every known cure over many years, but everything seemed to have a negative effect, and the hair loss accelerated. Eventually she realized her greatest fear: she was completely bald. Every doctor confirmed that the condition was irreversible. Her only options were painful hair transplants or to wear a wig. She refused to accept this and so she placed signs all around her room saying, "Thank you for my natural, black, beautiful hair." She sketched herself with a healthy head of hair, and she repeated over and over, "Thank you for my healing." This was in 2008. Initially it was difficult for her to match her feelings with her words, but she persisted, and within a few months she began to really feel the truth of her words, even though physically nothing had changed. By 2009, the first signs of patchy hair started to regrow. And just three years later her hair was fully regrown—long, thick, and natural.

Let's be grateful for healthy hair!

Another woman's overall kidney function was down to 30 percent and failing fast. This woman held a dream of living a full and energetic life with her family, and so she refused to accept the negative prognosis. Every day and night she would endeavor to feel, believe, and know that she was healing, and most importantly, to be truly grateful for her health. Her doctors, along with a panel of kidney specialists, were baffled by her swift and full recovery, which she put down to an attitude of gratitude.

Let's be grateful for our healthy kidneys!

A young couple's dreams of expanding their family were shattered tragically when their son was stillborn. Very soon after, the wife contracted an illness that shut down her reproductive system. She and her husband were told that she would be unable to have any more children. Though still grieving their loss, they took matters into their own hands. Every morning, they thanked the universe for being pregnant, even though they were not. They would then list all the things they were grateful for, focusing entirely upon the positive. Within a year, and contrary to all the best medical opinions, they managed to become pregnant once more—with a boy and a girl, their miracle twins.

Let's be grateful for life!

The Healing Power of Gratitude

Gratitude *increases* the natural flow of health to the mind and body, and can assist the body in healing more quickly, as countless studies have shown. The power of gratitude also works hand in hand with good bodily care, nutrition, and any medical assistance you might have chosen to follow.

When there is some kind of sickness in your body, it is understandable that you may have negative feelings about it, like stress, worry, frustration, or fear. But having negative feelings about sickness does not restore health. In fact, it has the opposite effect—it reduces health even more. To increase your health, you need to replace the negative feelings with good feelings, and gratitude is the easiest way to do it.

Being grateful for your health ensures that you will continue to receive more health to be grateful for, and at the same time it eliminates stress and tension in your body and mind. Scientific research has shown that stress is at the root of many diseases. Studies have also revealed that people who practice gratitude heal faster, and are likely to live seven years longer!

It makes perfect sense why this would be so, as according to the law of attraction whatever you are grateful for multiplies. It's simple math. The degree that you are grateful for your health is the exact degree that your health will increase, and the degree that you're not grateful is the exact degree that your health will decrease. When you practice gratitude, you will begin to see the improvements to your health happen right away. Little aches and pains, moles, scars, or marks will start to magically disappear, and you will notice your energy, vitality, and happiness increase markedly.

You may be sick or unwell now, or even in a lot of pain, but you are still continuing to receive the gift of health, and you can be grateful for that. It can be very difficult to access feelings of gratitude when you're sick or in pain, but even the smallest bit of gratitude helps increase the flow of health to the body.

On the other hand, when you're focused on something you don't like about your body, you are not being grateful for your body. Think about it. By the law of attraction, complaints about your body bring more problems to complain about, and so complaining about your body or appearance puts your very health at risk.

Be grateful for your body instead of finding fault with it. Every time you have a thought of something you don't like about your body, remember that all of the cells inside your body share your feelings and respond accordingly. Instead, say *thank you* with all your heart for what you do like about your body, and ignore the things you don't like.

Gratitude for Your Magnificent Body

Think about all the parts of your body that you truly appreciate and love.

Think about your legs and feet; they are your main form of transportation in your life. Think about all the things you use your legs for, like balancing, standing up, sitting down, exercising, dancing, climbing steps, driving a car, and most of all, the miracle of walking. The ability to walk gives us freedom to enjoy life! Say, "Thank you for my legs and feet," and really mean it.

Think about your arms and hands and how many things you pick up and hold in one day. Your hands are the major tools of your life, and they are in nonstop use all day long, every day. Say, "Thank you for my arms, hands, and fingers!"

Think about your amazing senses. Your sense of taste gives you so much pleasure multiple times throughout the day as you eat and drink. Say, "Thank you for my amazing sense of taste!"

Your sense of smell enables you to experience the beautiful fragrances of life. Say, "Thank you for my wonderful sense of smell!"

Your sense of touch allows you to touch your loved ones with a reassuring hug, and to feel the touch of a hand from one human being to another is one of the most precious things in life. Say, "Thank you for my precious sense of touch!"

Think about the miracle of your eyes, which enable you to see the faces of your loved ones and friends, read printed books, newspapers, and emails, watch television, see the beauty of nature, and most importantly, see your way through life. Say, "Thank you for my eyes that enable me to see everything!"

Without ears and your sense of hearing you could not use a phone, hear music, listen to the radio, hear your loved ones talk, or hear any of the sounds of the world around you. Say, "Thank you for my hearing!"

And to use any of your senses would be impossible without your brain, which processes over a million messages a second through all of your senses! It is actually your brain that enables you to sense and experience life, and there is no computer technology in the world that can duplicate it. Say, "Thank you for my brain and my beautiful mind!"

Think about your life-sustaining organs, which are continuously filtering, cleaning, and renewing everything in your body, and think about the fact that they do all their work automatically without you even having to think about it. Say, "Thank you organs, for working perfectly!" Think about your amazing immune system that works so hard to keep you well and heal you. Say, "Thank you, immune system!"

But more miraculous than any sense, system, function, or other organ in our body is the organ of your heart. Your heart governs the life of every other organ, because it is your heart that keeps the life flowing to every system in your body. Say, "Thank you for my strong and healthy heart!"

Your entire body is the greatest laboratory on the planet, and there's nothing that can come even close to replicating its magnificence. You are a miracle!

Say, "Thank you for my magnificent body!"

Gratitude for Food

Another powerful way to use gratitude in relation to your health is to give thanks for the food that you put into your body.

Giving thanks for food before you eat is a tradition that has been followed for thousands of years, dating back to the ancient Egyptians, who believed that when they blessed their food and water with gratitude it purified whatever they were blessing.

With the fast pace of life in the twenty-first century, taking the time to give thanks for a meal has more often than not been left behind. But when you look at the theories and discoveries that quantum physics has made in recent times, such as the observer effect, the ancient Egyptians may very well have been right. The observer effect in quantum physics refers to changes that the act of observation makes in whatever is being observed. Imagine if focusing gratitude on your food and drinks changed their energy structure, and purified them so that everything you consumed had the ultimate effect of well-being in your body? Well, this is exactly what happens when you bless your food—you change the structure of the food and its effect on your body. Blessing water with love and gratitude does the same thing.

You need food to live, to think, to feel good, and to maintain your health, and so there is a *great* deal to be grateful for about food.

Before you eat or drink anything today, whether you're about to eat a meal, a piece of fruit, a snack, or have a drink of anything, including water, take a moment to look at what you're about to eat or drink, and in your mind or out loud say the words, "Thank you!" *Really* feel the love and gratitude. Also, make sure your conversations are positive when you are sitting down to a meal. And if you can, take at least one mouthful really savoring your food; it will not only increase your enjoyment of it, it will also increase your health and well-being.

A woman wrote to me describing her struggle in being considerably overweight. Despite strict dieting and working out in the gym every day, she had not managed to shed a single pound. That's when she decided to try something new. She began to eat more consciously. She would bless her food before she took a bite; she would savor it, and she would pray that it nourished her body. The effect was almost instant. She stopped craving food and obsessing over food, and she worried less about what was healthy and what could make her put on weight. She simply ate what she wanted when she wanted. She wrote up a list of all the things she was grateful for, and she also expressed gratitude for all the things she would be able to do once she reached her target weight. This included fitting into her dream wedding gown. Within a month she managed to lose more than a third of her body weight and was well on her way to her ideal size. This was all thanks to her newfound gratitude and appreciation for food and for herself.

Let's be grateful for food and the good health it provides!

Gratitude is the great multiplier, so say *thank you* for your health every single day. All the money in the world cannot buy health, because it is a gift from life, and so more than anything else, be grateful for your health! Your gratitude is a guarantee that your health will continue to get better and better.

LESSON 6

VISUALIZING HEALTH

Very often when a person is diagnosed with an illness or disease of some kind, they will not only worry about it a lot, but they will research the disease, gathering information about its possible worsening symptoms and dreaded outcomes. In other words, they give their entire focus to the disease.

However, the law of attraction says that we can't make a problem go away by focusing on it, because focusing on the problem can only make the problem worse. Instead, we should do the exact opposite, and focus on the *ideal* state for the area of our body that is unwell, and give our thoughts and feelings to that. Focusing on or *visualizing* the ideal state of any part of our body powerfully uses our thoughts and feelings together so we magnetize it to us in one fell swoop!

Visualizing is a process that has been taught by all the great teachers and avatars throughout the centuries, as well as by all the great teachers living today. The reason visualizing health is so powerful is because as you create pictures in your mind of seeing yourself well, you are generating thoughts and feelings of *being* well right now. Visualizing is simply powerfully focused thought in pictures, and it causes equally powerful feelings. When you are visualizing, you are emitting that powerful frequency out into the Universe. The law of attraction will take hold of that powerful visualization and return those pictures back to you, just as you saw them in your mind.

How can it be that the mind has so much power to change physical things? Ancient traditions tell us emphatically that everything—absolutely everything—we perceive in the physical world is made of "mind." They say that all matter is actually "mind stuff," and that is why the mind can change anything.

Picture Your Perfect Body

As you see the picture in your mind and feel it, you are bringing yourself to a place of believing you have it now. Your subconscious mind does not know whether you are imagining something or whether it is real. Remember, the subconscious mind governs all aspects of your body and your health. When you imagine perfect health, and believe you have it, the subconscious mind receives those thoughts and images as though you actually have it, and through the law of attraction, it must return those images to you.

The goal is to focus on the end result and experience the feeling of that, without giving any attention whatsoever to "how" it will come about. When you are in the place where what you are imagining feels real, you will know that it has penetrated your subconscious mind, and the law of attraction must deliver it. Your picture in your mind is seeing it as done. Your feelings are seeing it as done. Your mind and your entire state of being are seeing it as *already happened*. That is the art of visualization.

One woman had tried to quit smoking many times but had never managed to last a single day. Her problem was she couldn't even think

*of her life without cigarettes, and that's exactly
what was keeping her smoking. So she started to
visualize and to imagine what her days would
look like healthy and free from smoking. The
result was that she managed to break the habit
and she never smoked another cigarette. It turned
out to be so much easier than she had thought it
would be, and that is because any addiction of the
body is no match for the power of imagination
and the law of attraction.*

*Let's be grateful for the pure, clean air that we
breathe into our lungs!*

Visualization for Perfect Health

When Denis Waitley first introduced us to
visualization in the documentary version of *The
Secret*, he told us that if you can go there in the
mind, you can go there in the body. He and his
colleagues established through scientific research
that the body cannot distinguish between what is
imagined and what is real, so it responds the same
either way. Consider the health ramifications of
that alone. Dr. Waitley famously took visualization
from the Apollo space program and introduced it
to Olympic athletes in the 1980s and '90s. Think
about the superhuman feats of strength and

endurance achieved with the aid of visualization by athletes like champion swimmer Michael Phelps. Using these same methods, you too can achieve your perfect state of health through the power of your imagination.

Visualizing your perfect health is a very simple process.

Spend one minute in visualizing a scene of yourself with the *ideal* state of your body that you want. And as you see your body in your mind the way you want it to be, be grateful for it as though you have received it.

If you want to restore health to an injured back, picture yourself with a strong and healthy back, one that supports your whole body and provides you with unhindered mobility. Then feel gratitude as though you have already received it. If you want to restore health to an upset stomach, imagine yourself feeling perfectly at ease as your stomach digests food effortlessly and helps deliver vital nutrients to all parts of your body. If you want to restore health to your heart, then visualize a strong and healthy heart pumping efficiently and maintaining the well-being of every organ in your body.

If you want to improve your eyesight, then imagine yourself seeing clearly. If you want to improve your hearing, then imagine hearing everything perfectly. If you want more flexibility, then see yourself with a perfectly supple and agile body. If you want to change your weight, first think about the *ideal* weight that you want to be, then visualize yourself at that ideal weight, and give thanks for it as though you have received it now.

Whatever it is that you want to improve, first imagine yourself with the *ideal* state, and then be grateful for the *ideal* state as though you have received it already.

A sixteen-year-old girl did exactly that after she was involved in a terrible motorcycle accident. Though she had no recall of the actual incident, she did remember a doctor saying that she might die due to the number of fractures to her face and head. She had suffered sixty wounds to her face, requiring multiple surgeries to her mouth, nose, and jaw. She was advised that recuperation would be slow and painful, and that long-term scarring was inevitable. However, this girl quite literally saw things differently. She visualized herself living her normal life and going out with friends, but with a face completely free of scars. In fact, she imagined herself having the most beautiful face in the world, and gave thanks to the Universe as though it were already true. Her doctors were amazed by how quickly and how well she was able to recuperate. Within twenty days, she was back home, happy, and healthy. It is now several years since the accident, but there is no sign of it on her face—the scars are gone. She is exactly as she imagined herself.

Let's give thanks for our health and safety!

Visualization Creates Miracles

Nothing is impossible, and there is no such thing as a hopeless situation. No matter what the odds, healing is always possible. Think of the story about Morris Goodman in the film of *The Secret*. After surviving an airplane crash, Morris lay in the hospital completely paralyzed, only able to blink his eyes. His doctors told him he would never walk again. But Morris knew the power within him to bring about what he chose to think about. He knew he could still use his mind to visualize, and, against all odds, Morris walked out through the hospital doors.

If you are injured or ill, but things are not improving, it means you're imagining and feeling the injury or illness more than you're imagining and feeling a full recovery. You have to tip the balance the other way. Fill yourself with good thoughts and good feelings about making a full recovery, or about anything and everything that makes you feel good. Feel good as much as you can, because every moment of good feelings brings a full recovery.

When you imagine and feel having what you want, you're literally in a new world with what you've imagined, so don't contradict the new world by telling everyone about an injury or illness that's not improving, because then you are imagining the worst again, and you're back in the old world. As you imagine the worst, that's what you will receive back. As you imagine the best, that's what you'll receive back. The fact that you can imagine a full recovery means that it already exists! If somebody asks how you are doing, you can say, "I am *feeling* one hundred percent again and my body is following." Or you can say, "This has been a blessing because it has made me appreciate my body and health more than I ever have in my life." Or if you are bold enough, you can say, "I have a full recovery by the horns."

Visualizing for Others

Visualizing good health for others is also possible. Just like my friend Marcy did for her husband, if you want to help someone who is having problems with their health, you can visualize in your mind the person being strong, happy, and healthy. To do this effectively, create a scene in your mind with you and the person, and put as much detail into the scene as possible. Imagine the words you are both saying, and see the person doing things that only a happy and healthy person can do. Play that scene over and over and feel your visualization deeply, as though you are really living it. Although ultimately the person is creating their own life, this process can help them immeasurably if they want to be well again. It is even more powerful if you can encourage them to join you in visualizing together.

A young mother experienced this for herself when her partner was undertaking some home renovations and accidentally severed three of his fingers. The surgeon was reluctant to attempt reattachment as the nerve damage was extreme. Given that the man worked with his hands, this was essentially a career-ending prognosis. The couple insisted that the surgeon do his best to reattach the fingers. However, the man was given little chance of the fingers healing and much less of them fully recovering. But the woman would hear no such negativity as she set about imagining her partner's hand completely healed and fully functional. Together with her partner, their favorite dual visualization featured the two of them riding his Harley-Davidson motorcycle, his hand working the throttle with perfect dexterity.

Three days after the surgery, the bandages were removed and doctors were astonished by how well the hand had healed. By this stage, even the surgeon was starting to believe the man would make a full recovery. Indeed, he was back to work within six weeks, and at three months an X-ray revealed that missing bone fragments had regrown—he was practically as good as new. And perhaps most importantly, he was able to work the throttle on his Harley-Davidson to take him and his partner riding once again.

Let's be really grateful for our hands and fingers!

For parents, the ultimate challenge can be when their child's health appears to be in danger. But whatever Secret practices we can use to heal ourselves we can also use for our children. While you cannot override anyone else's experience if their journey is meant to take a different path, children are very receptive to positive thoughts and feelings.

One man wrote to us with a powerful story about the premature birth of his baby niece. When his sister-in-law fell seriously ill seven months into pregnancy, the doctor insisted that they induce labor immediately. The baby was given very little chance of survival. In fact, the situation was so dire that the doctor was asking whether to prioritize the life of the mother or the baby. That's when this man put his visualizing skills to the test. He imagined holding the baby while saying, "Thank you for the perfect health of both mother and child." He repeated this mantra over and over until his niece was delivered and the doctor assured them that they were out of the woods for now. Being two months premature, the baby was immediately placed in intensive care. Doctors were still a little pessimistic about her chances of surviving. But this family refused to take on any negativity. Instead of discussing the baby's condition, they went out and bought her baby clothes and they spent their time arguing over who she most resembled. Despite all the tubes and wires and medical apparatus connected to the tiny baby, every night before bed her uncle continued to visualize himself playing with his niece, holding her, and most importantly, seeing her in perfect health. Six weeks later, the family was able to take her home as she had fully recovered and was as healthy as any other newborn baby.

Let's be grateful for healthy families!

Imagine Health

No matter what the situation you might find yourself facing, try to imagine how you would feel fully healed.

If you can imagine being well, you will *feel* being well, and when you feel it to be true, you receive it. To see your health improve, all you have to do is imagine and feel what it would be like having the health you want in your body.

If you are overweight or underweight, and you visualize having the perfect weight right now, how do you feel? You feel different from how you've been feeling. Everything about you would change. You would walk differently, talk differently, and you would do things differently. Walk like that now! Talk like that now! Act as if you have it now! It doesn't matter what it is that you want; imagine how you would feel with it, and if you can, feel that way now. Whatever you imagine with feeling you are sending out, and by the law of attraction you must receive it.

Take your imagination with you every day, and *imagine* what it would be like *if* you were overflowing with health. *Imagine* how you would feel *if* you could do what you wanted to do. Use

all of your senses and imagine every scene and
situation you can with the health you want, and
feel that you have it now. Imagine the perfect
weight, the perfect body, the perfect health of
an organ, and feel having it. Feel the gratitude
for having it, and also be utterly grateful for all
the health you had already! Try spending three
minutes each day imagining and feeling having
the state of health you want. Do it each day until
you feel as though you already have it. Do it until
you know it belongs to you, as you know your
name belongs to you. With some changes to your
health, you will get to the desired state after just
one or two days. Other changes may take you
longer. Your body can change into whatever you
want, but it can only do it through your thoughts,
your feelings, and your imagination.

Health Vision Board

Another way that you can use your imagination
to attract perfect health is with the aid of a Vision
Board.

When you place pictures of what you want or how
you want your life to be on your Vision Board, it
helps you create the image in your mind of that
desired outcome. You can use old photographs

of yourself when you were at your most healthy and vibrant or engaging in activities that you wish you could do again. You can use old photos of yourself when you were the size that you'd like to return to. Alternately, you can use pictures of other people who are at your weight or health goal now, or people doing things that you have always wished you could do. Make sure you put your Vision Board in a place where you will see it and look at it every day. As you look at the Vision Board, you are imprinting the picture of your desire in your mind, and as you focus on your Vision Board it stimulates your senses and evokes a positive feeling within you. *Feel* the feelings of having and being and doing those things now. Then you have the two elements of creation—your mind and your feelings—working in full force.

I know of a woman who was struggling to get pregnant with her second child, and over a period of three and a half years, she suffered through six miscarriages. Understandably, she started to blame and doubt herself. This situation was not helped by doctors and other fertility experts making a point of her advancing age and everything else that was "wrong" with her. Worse still, she didn't have enough money or health insurance funds to cover IVF treatment or other expensive fertility treatments. The dream of a second baby began to fade.

At this time, she decided to focus on her first child and be grateful for this blessing. Her gratitude brought about a dramatic change to her circumstances. Her employer was bought out, and the new owner provided medical insurance that included coverage for IVF. She was also required to change doctors, and her new fertility expert was much more optimistic about her becoming pregnant.

In the early stages of the treatment program, she decided to create a Vision Board. She included a picture she had found online of a cute baby that shared physical attributes with both her husband and herself. She hung that picture over her desk so that she was sure to see it every day.

Despite the support and encouragement of her new doctor, the IVF procedure did not go entirely to plan. As a result, they had only one egg available for fertilization. On the day of transfer, a nurse gave her a picture of her eight-cell embryo, and the joy and hope brought the woman to tears. She would later add this picture to her Vision Board alongside the picture of the baby she had found online. Given her history of miscarriage, it would be a long shot for this one and only embryo to implant and for her to carry this pregnancy to term. But that's exactly what happened, and nine months later, her happy, healthy son was born.

The family relocated shortly after the baby was born, but several months later the new mom was unpacking boxes when she came across her Vision Board. She was stunned. The cute baby in the picture she had taken from the internet was the spitting image of her now fifteen-month-old baby boy.

Let's be grateful for miracles!

So take inspiration from this woman and don't ever be discouraged by a tough prognosis, or suggestions that something is impossible. I like to say that *anything* is possible if you believe.

The fact is, your entire life up to now is what you have *imagined* it to be. Everything you have or don't have, every situation and circumstance of your life, including your health, your abilities, and your limitations—all are what you have imagined into existence. Instead of imagining the best, many people are in fear and imagine all the things that can go wrong, and as surely as they keep imagining and feeling those things, they happen. Feel and imagine the very best and the highest you can for your health and your body, and for every area of your life, because the best you can imagine is a piece of cake for you and the law of attraction!

LESSON 7

AFFIRMING HEALTH

One of the things that people often do when they have an illness is talk about it all the time. That's because they're thinking about it all the time, so they're just verbalizing their thoughts. If you are feeling a little unwell, don't talk about it—unless you want more of it. Disease is held in the body by thought, by observation of the illness, and by the attention given to the illness.

One woman who wrote in to us said her allergies were so bad that she always seemed to be suffering from a cough or cold brought on by sudden changes in the weather, dust in the air, or even fragrances. And whenever she felt one of these allergy attacks coming on, she would automatically discuss it with her family and friends. Eventually she came to realize it was this negative energy created by talking about her issue that held the condition of allergies to her and caused her suffering. She immediately stopped discussing her health problems with friends and family, and before long, she managed to rid herself of all symptoms.

Let's be grateful for feeling healthy and well!

If you are feeling a little unwell, accept that your thoughts and words were responsible and repeat as often as you can, "I feel wonderful. I feel so good," and really feel it. If you are not feeling great and somebody asks you how you are feeling, just be grateful that that person has reminded you to think thoughts of feeling well. Speak only the words of what you want.

Talking about a virus that's going around, fatigue, aches and pains, symptoms of the flu, or a diagnosis that you've just received from your doctor, is talking about what you don't want. Every time you get caught up in talking about what you don't want, you bring more struggle and difficulty to your life. When you talk about any difficulties with your health, you are not talking about what you want.

Talk about how good it is to be full of health. Talk about the energy you have and all you plan to do with it. Talk about the things you're grateful for concerning your body and your health. You have to talk about what you want to bring to you. In conversations and in your thoughts say, "Imagine if . . . ," and then fill in the rest of the sentence with what you want. "Imagine if I had the energy I had when I was twenty again," "Imagine if I woke up each day excited to get out of bed."

If you're talking to a friend and they're complaining about their health, help them by saying, "Imagine if you were one hundred percent recovered. Imagine how you would feel!" Because the truth is, the possibility of your friend being perfectly healthy already exists, and if they can imagine and feel it, they can receive it! However, if you cannot turn the conversation in a positive direction, then simply excuse yourself and be on your way. As you walk away, give your powerful thoughts and feelings to seeing your friend well, and then let it go.

Affirmations for Perfect Health

When it comes to your own life, however, you can change anything, because you have an unlimited ability to think and talk about what you want. Therefore, you have an unlimited ability to bring everything good in life to you, including perfect health! One of the fastest and most direct ways to do this is through affirmations. An affirmation is like a personal mission statement that you say to yourself over and over again until it sinks into your subconscious as a belief. Remember, the subconscious mind governs all aspects of your body and your health. Therefore, when a health affirmation turns into a subconscious belief, it becomes a command from your subconscious mind to all of your cells and organs to stimulate healing.

> *There was a woman who described herself as negative and depressed. She was overweight and hated her body, and she believed that whenever she experienced good times there were bad times sure to come. In this light, she went to a gynecologist's appointment where she received some distressing news: her cells were abnormal and she was just one step away from cervical cancer. They told her she would need urgent surgery to remove these abnormal*

cells. *In the meantime, she made the decision to regain control of her life. She quit smoking and went to a personal trainer to get fit and lose a few pounds. But most importantly, day and night, she would say to herself, "I am healthy, I feel healthy!" Within a couple of days of telling herself "I am healthy, I feel healthy!" she actually started to believe it. From that point on, she just knew she would be okay. On the day of surgery, a miracle happened. A new biopsy of the affected cells revealed absolutely no signs of abnormality or cancer. This was in stark contrast to the two previous biopsies. Her doctor said that in forty-five years of practicing medicine, he had never seen anything like it. He said it was as if her cells had healed themselves. But of course, that's exactly what had happened. Her powerful affirmation, "I am healthy, I feel healthy!" acted as a command to her body to heal itself.*

Let's be grateful for all of our healthy cells!

The Power of "I Am"

This simple affirmation, "I am healthy," reveals the great secret to affirmations in the first two words: "I AM!"

When you say, "I am," the words that follow are summoning creation with a mighty force, because you are declaring it to be fact. You are stating it with certainty. And so immediately after you say, "I am tired," or "I am sick," or "I am hurting," or "I am overweight," or "I am old," Genie says, "Your wish is my command."

Knowing this, wouldn't it be a good idea to begin to use the two most powerful words, "I AM," to your advantage? How about, "I AM happy," "I AM healthy," "I AM strong," "I AM youthful," "I AM filled with energy every single day."

In his book *The Master Key System*, Charles Haanel claims that there is an affirmation that incorporates every single thing any human being can want, and that this affirmation will bring about harmonious conditions to all things. He adds, *"The reason for this is because the affirmation is in strict accordance with the Truth, and when Truth appears every form of error or discord must necessarily disappear."*

The affirmation is this: "I am whole, perfect, strong, powerful, loving, harmonious, and happy."

Try using this affirmation every day.

"I am whole, perfect, strong, powerful, loving, harmonious, and happy."

Of course, the effective use of affirmations depends entirely on how much you believe them when you say them. If there is no belief, then the affirmation is just words that have no power. If you find you're having trouble believing, constant repetition of your affirmations will help to build your belief. And when you finally believe what you say, you just created it, no matter what it is.

If you are currently dealing with a health issue, whenever you remember, at any time of the day, say, "I am well." Say it hundreds of times a day if you like. Say it often, but say it very, very slowly, giving equal emphasis to each word. "I—am—well." Feel the meaning of the words as you slowly say them, and experience as much of a feeling of wellness within you as you can. Build on that feeling every single day. You will get better and better at it. Feel that wellness inside you more than you react to outside circumstances, and you will change the outside circumstances.

A schoolteacher applied this practice to overcome depression, something he had experienced a number of times over many years. When the latest episode struck, he fell to a new low. But rather than continue to suffer, he would repeat to himself over and over the affirmative statement "I am healing." He followed this up with the more specific affirmation "I will find the right therapist and I will heal." These two simple affirmations proved to be a success—he found the right doctor, and set himself on the path to good mental health.

A young woman shared a similar experience. She suffered from chronic depression and an anxiety disorder, and had been taking antidepressant medication for five years. Every time she attempted to wean herself off the drugs, she would get severe heart palpitations, and the fear and anxiety would see her straight back on the medication. So she turned to affirmations. Inspired by a story she read on the Secret website, she affirmed: "My body and my neurons can produce all the chemicals and neurotransmitters to heal myself." She followed this up by saying: "Thank you for my healing." She repeated these two affirmations all day long, so desperate was she to heal herself. She slept well that night and awoke the next morning deciding not to medicate. There were no palpitations and no negative thoughts all through the next day. Months later, she is free of all symptoms of depression and anxiety, and she experienced no withdrawal symptoms as a result of going off her medication. Best of all, she is happy for the first time in years, and it is all thanks to positive thoughts and affirmations.

Let's all of us give thanks for our mental health!

While it may seem incredible that something like chronic depression could be cured overnight, know that the body is fully capable of producing all of the neurochemicals, proteins, antigens, and immune cells necessary to balance and overcome any condition, including mental illness. Just remember that any decision to stop or adjust medication should be made in consultation with a medical professional.

A Powerful Autosuggestion

In the 1900s, Émile Coué (a French psychologist and pharmacist) was a pioneer in the work of using positive thoughts to aid in healing. Part of his successful healing methods involved the simple daily application by his patients of this conscious autosuggestion:

"Every day, in every way, I am getting better and better."

This is not only a powerful statement for health. As you can see by the words, it is a powerful statement for all areas of our life. When using this affirmation say it very slowly and with the full conviction of the meaning of the words. It is the energy we put into words that makes them powerful.

Your job is to imagine perfect health, and then repeat that thought over and over in your mind until it becomes a belief. The Universe will then take up your cause, inspiring people, circumstances, and events to come together to make you well.

> *This is what occurred to a young woman who was diagnosed with multiple sclerosis, an autoimmune disorder that affects the brain and spinal cord. There is no known cause for MS, and there is no known cure. The prognosis of the disease varies, but for this woman it was particularly aggressive. Just eighteen months after her first diagnosis, she was already becoming disabled on one side of her body. That's when she put her powerful affirmation to work. If anyone asked, she would tell them, "I am perfectly healthy!" Even if they didn't ask, she would still tell them, "I am perfectly healthy!" And she did everything she could to help her believe her affirmation, including visualization and prayer.*

> *Two months later, she attended a seminar on multiple sclerosis, hoping to pick up some useful yoga tips. She was initially disheartened to see most of the other people in attendance in wheelchairs. Nevertheless, she met a guest*

speaker who lectured on the latest developments in stem cell transplants. It turned out that at her stage of the disease, this treatment could stop the progression of MS. This meant that she would not suffer any further side effects, and it would, in effect, be a cure. The only problem now was that this treatment was unavailable in her country—she would have to travel overseas, it was prohibitively expensive, and there was a two- to three-year waiting list.

Undeterred, she went back to her affirmative thoughts of perfect health, and visualized her healthy body. She also thanked the Universe for receiving her stem cell treatment from the best doctor in the best hospital at an affordable price.

A few months later, she was delighted to learn that the treatment was about to be made available in her country at a heavily subsidized price. Better still, she was to be the very first patient. The treatment was such an unprecedented success, and the side effects so minimal, that she was discharged from the hospital a whole week ahead of schedule. She has since become an advocate for stem cell transplants, offering counseling to MS patients all around the world.

There can be no disputing that this woman benefitted tremendously from access to cutting-

edge medical treatment. However, it is also true that she attracted this procedure and this life-saving opportunity through the power of her thoughts and words.

Let's give thanks for great advances in medical science!

You have the power to create anything you want, because you are much more than a human being; you are an Infinite Being. Perfect health is who you are, and it is fully available to your body now. You don't actually have to create it, because it's penetrating every cell of your body constantly. You just have to stop doing what you're doing that's preventing health from manifesting in your body now. Under no circumstances entertain thoughts of illness, and under every circumstance focus on thoughts of health and well-being.

To conclude this lesson, I would like to share with you a list of my favorite health affirmations, which I use most days. I recommend that you choose at least twenty-five of these affirmations to recite to yourself daily. If you're facing a particular situation with your health, then I would suggest doing all of them every day. It's what I do. You can also choose the ones that resonate with you and best suit the health you want to manifest.

My Favorite Health Affirmations

All is well.
I am well.
My body is well.
Health is all there is.
Health is here now.
Health is who I am.
I am healthy, healthy, healthy.
I am whole, perfect, strong, powerful, loving,
    harmonious, and happy.
Thank you for my body's perfect health.
I am fighting fit.
I am as fit as a fiddle with energy to spare.
I am full of beans.
I am as strong as an ox.
I am hale and hearty.
I am in great shape.
I am fit and well.
I have a clean bill of health.
I am a picture of good health.
My body is in perfect balance and perfect health.
I am thinking positively which allows full health
    to flow through my body.
My body is 100 percent perfectly well.
My body is in complete harmony.
I am manifesting perfect stability in my body.
I can see clearly.
I can hear clearly.

My hearing is perfect.

My balance is perfect.

My bones are strong.

Every morning when I wake my body is fully rested, relaxed, and energized.

I am grateful for the ever-increasing health of my body.

I feel fantastic.

I feel amazing.

I am well. I am well. I am well.

I am living a long, long, long, happy, happy, happy, healthy, healthy life.

Thank you, thank you, thank you for my perfect health and well-being.

LESSON 8

THE IMMORTAL YOU

The Nobel Prize–winning quantum physicist Richard Feynman once said, *"There is nothing in biology yet found that indicates the inevitability of death. This suggests . . . that it is not at all inevitable and that it is only a matter of time before biologists discover what it is that is causing us the trouble."*

Ancient texts say that people once lived for hundreds and hundreds of years. Some lived for eight hundred years, some lived for five or six hundred years, but longevity was commonplace. So what's happened? People changed what they believed. Instead of believing in living for hundreds and hundreds of years, people changed their beliefs over generations, and they came to believe in a reduced life expectancy.

We have inherited those beliefs of a reduced life expectancy, as well as beliefs about the inevitability of sickness and the body deteriorating. From the time we are born, the belief of how long we can live and how the body changes through time is sewn into the fabric of our subconscious minds. And from there we literally program our bodies from an early age to live for a certain amount of time, and our bodies age and deteriorate according to how we program them.

If you possibly can, don't put a ceiling on how long you can live. All it will take is one person to break the limits of life expectancy, and that person will change the course of life expectancy for all humanity. One person after another will follow, because when one person lives far beyond the current life expectancy, other people will believe and feel they can do it too, and they will!

You Are Eternal

In truth, there *are no* limits, and certainly not ones imposed by your health, your body, or even your death. Many human beings have such a fear of death, but the truth is, the body may end but we are *eternal life*. On a physical level we are pure energy.

What does this mean? Well, when you break it down, everything in the Universe is made of energy, including you. Starting with your body, you have your limbs and your organs, then your cells, then molecules, and then atoms. And then at the subatomic level, everything becomes energy. You are made of pure energy.

How does all of this make you eternal? For me, the answer to that question is one of the most magnificent parts of the teachings of The Secret. You are energy, and it is known conclusively through science that energy can never be created or destroyed, it can only change form. And that means you! The true essence of you, the pure energy of you, has always been and always will be. You can never *not* be.

On a deep level, you know that. Can you imagine not being? Despite everything you have seen and experienced in your life, can you imagine not being? You cannot imagine it, because it is impossible. A human being cannot imagine *not* existing. We can imagine our body not being alive, but we simply cannot imagine not existing. Why do you think that is? Do you think it's a fluke? It's not. You cannot imagine yourself not existing because it's impossible for you not to exist! If you could imagine it, you could create it, and you can never create it! You have always existed and you will always exist because you are a part of creation. You are eternal energy.

So what happens when a person dies? The body doesn't go into nonexistence, because there's no such thing. It integrates itself into the elements. And the being that is inside you—the *real* you— doesn't go into nonexistence either. The very word "being" tells you that you will always be! When you die, you don't become a human "been," and likewise, before birth, you are not referred to as a human "about to be"! You are an eternal being having a temporary human experience. If you stopped existing, there would be an empty space in the universe, and the whole universe would collapse into that empty space.

Another way I like to look at it is that we are intelligent enough to trade in an old car when it is not serving its purpose anymore. We hand over the old car, and we take possession of a newer model and continue our journey in our new car. The greater part of you is also intelligent enough to trade in the vehicle of your body when it is not serving its purpose anymore, update to a newer, better model, and continue on your journey in the new vehicle. Human bodies and cars are both vehicles and you are the eternal driver.

You can experience unlimited health and happiness in this body and this life, but never forget that you are eternal life expressing itself as you. You are the infinite being. You are all power. You are all wisdom. You are all intelligence. You are perfection. You are magnificence. You are the creator, and you are creating the creation of you on this planet.

A Summary of

The Secret to Health

Now that you know The Secret, you have at your command the power to change anything, including your health. Through your own thoughts, and using the Creative Process and other powerful processes discussed in this book, you can choose to overcome disease, ward off sickness, recover from injury, improve your fitness, achieve your ideal body size, or maintain eternal youth. It's up to you.

Your job is quite simply to get clear on what you want and be prepared for the Universe to provide the way. Don't try to predict or force the solution, and be open to all solutions. Remain focused on the end result of health, not on *how* you're going to achieve its restoration. The law of attraction operates on the inside of you. It's responding to your thoughts. This is where your power lies.

We're so used to running around taking action to try and figure out problems, fix them, or eliminate them. We're so used to focusing on our problems, but now you know that if you want to free yourself of problems, including health problems, take your mind off the problem and fixate on what you want! You have infinite power in the outside world, but the way to it is through what you choose to focus on.

As Australian wellness expert James Duigan says: *"If you don't like something, take away its only power: Your attention."*

Finally, I want to reiterate the importance of incorporating professional healthcare advice from a certified medical practitioner. Let your chosen practitioner attend to the symptoms and the physical manifestation of disease while you take care of the root cause of all sickness and healing— your thoughts and feelings. You have within you the most powerful self-healing capacity, and when it's used in concert with the wonders of medicine—traditional or alternative—you will be able to live to your greatest potential.

May the joy and well-being be with you.

Rhonda Byrne

THE SECRET
TO MONEY

INTRODUCTION
THE SECRET TO MONEY

Before I discovered The Secret, I was climbing the ladder of success in the television industry. I was living in a beautiful apartment, driving a nice car, and running a successful company of my own. After many years of struggle and sacrifice, I thought I'd finally made it—I was set for life. But then suddenly one devastating circumstance after another happened, and within a few short months my entire life had collapsed around me. My company was teetering on the brink of failure, and everything I'd worked so hard for was slipping from my grasp. I fell into despair, but it was in this very moment that I discovered a secret that not only saved my company but changed everything about my life.

I came to learn that this *secret* had been known by the greatest and most successful individuals throughout history. The knowledge they held allowed them to concentrate the vast majority of the world's wealth in the hands of very few.

As I began to integrate this knowledge into my own life, I developed a completely different mindset around money that radically changed the circumstances of money in my life. I know that anything I can do, you can do too, and once you understand the principles, you will be able to change your financial circumstances.

Whether you were born in India, the United States, Germany, or Africa, the circumstances of your beginnings do not dictate the kind of life you can have. It's not the conditions of your community or the outside world that determine whether or not your dreams will be fulfilled. Nor does it matter how much money you were born into, how educated you are, who you know, or how much experience you have. Once you put this knowledge into practice, you'll be able to fulfill all your dreams, be financially free, and never have to worry about money again. You will begin to feel what it's like to enjoy the freedom of unlimited wealth—your birthright.

The Secret to Money is your key to the life you have always wanted and the life you deserve. All good things are your birthright, and The Secret to Money will guide you in creating whatever you want. Welcome to the magic of life!

LESSON 1

THE SECRET TO MONEY

What is the secret to money?

That really is the million dollar question, because once you discover the secret to money, you will know the secret to life.

That's not to suggest that money is the most important thing in life—far from it. But when you know The Secret, you will be aware that you can have *anything* you want in life, including happiness, health, great relationships, and of course, plenty of money.

Prosperity is your birthright, and in every area of your life you hold the key to more abundance than you can possibly imagine. And in fact, anytime you imagine yourself living in abundance, you are actually determining your life through this most powerful natural law—the law of attraction.

What Is the Law of Attraction?

The Secret is the law of attraction.

It is the law that determines the complete order in the Universe, every moment of your life, and every single thing you experience in your life. It is a universal law, as impartial and impersonal as the law of gravity. And just like gravity, the law of attraction is always in effect—it is always happening. It doesn't matter who you are or where you are, the law of attraction is forming your entire life experience. And whether you know it or not, you are the one who calls the law of attraction into action, and you do it entirely through the magnetic power of your thoughts.

When you focus your thoughts on something, and you hold that focus, you are in that moment summoning the thing you are thinking about with the mightiest power in the Universe. Through this most powerful law, your thoughts become the things in your life. *Your thoughts become things.* Say this over to yourself and let it seep into your consciousness and your awareness:

Your thoughts become things!

You are like a magnet, and you attract all of the circumstances and events of your life. When you become a magnet of wealth, you attract wealth. When you become a magnet of health, you attract health. When you become a magnet of love, you attract love. You magnetize and receive the circumstances of wealth, health, love, relationships, your job, and every single event and experience in your life, based on what you are thinking. Think positive thoughts about money, and you magnetize positive circumstances, people, and events that bring more money to you. Think negative thoughts about money, and you magnetize negative circumstances, people, and events that cause you to have a lack of money. The law of attraction is unfailingly giving you every single thing in your life based on what you're thinking. When you think, "I can't afford it," then by law you will continue to experience not being able to afford things. If you think, "I don't have enough money," then most surely you will continue to not have enough money.

The Universal Supply

Like all the laws of nature, there is utter perfection in this law. You create your life. Whatever you sow, you reap! Your thoughts are seeds, and the harvest you reap will depend on the seeds you plant.

Think of the law of attraction as the law of supply. It is the law that enables you to draw from the universal supply. The Universe is the universal supplier of everything. Everything comes from the Universe, and is delivered to you through people, circumstances, and events, by the law of attraction. When you think about what you want, the perfect people, circumstances, and events will be delivered for you to receive it. Here's an example:

> *A woman in her early thirties wrote to tell me about her dream to give back to the community and to help young people achieve their goals. She had made the decision to change careers and had gone back to school to become a teacher. While studying at night, she picked up work as a substitute teacher by day at a local inner-city high school. The pay was lousy, the class sizes horrendously large, and her students cursed her out and abused her on a daily basis. Meanwhile,*

she was struggling under the weight of crippling student loans and credit-card debt. She would often cry at night, overwhelmed by it all, yet she never lost sight of her dream. Then, an opportunity arose to teach at an English-language school in Japan. She was promised small class sizes of enthusiastic students, and she would also be provided with an apartment. She leapt at the chance. The only problem now was that she had to clear her debts amounting to almost $40,000 in order to make the move. So she applied the law of attraction, first by writing herself a check for $40,000. Then she withdrew $200 in cash and began counting it over and over until she reached $40,000. She did this every day until large sums of money actually started rolling in. Two weeks before she was due in Japan, she received a check from her grandmother for $12,000, just because she was proud of her. Then, she was informed that $17,000 in student loans were being forgiven because she had spent time teaching in a high-needs district. And finally, she received back pay out of the blue from an ex-employer who owed her $10,000 for work she had completed a decade earlier. In a matter of days, she had raised the money she needed, having attracted the perfect people, circumstances, and events to clear her debts so that she could travel to Japan and live her dream.

Now that you know that everything comes from the Universe and that the Universe is the supplier of all things through the law of attraction, you will be very careful to watch your thoughts when you are dealing with money. Your thoughts about money are either attracting money to you or keeping money away from you.

Attract Abundance Instead of Lack

People who have drawn wealth into their lives are using The Secret, whether consciously or unconsciously. They think thoughts of abundance and wealth, and they do not allow contradictory thoughts to take root in their minds. Their predominant thoughts are of wealth. They only know wealth, and scarcity doesn't exist in their minds. Whether they are aware of it or not, their predominant thoughts of wealth are what brought wealth to them. It is the law of attraction in action.

The reason any person does not have enough money is because they are *blocking* money from coming to them with their thoughts. Every negative thought is *blocking* your good from coming to you, and that includes money. It is not that the money is being kept from you by the Universe, because all the money you require exists right now in the invisible. If you do not have enough, it is because you are stopping the flow of money coming to you, and you are doing that with your thoughts. You must tip the balance of your thoughts from lack of money to more than enough money. Think more about abundance than about lack, and you have tipped the balance.

In a nutshell, as you think of yourself living in abundance, you are powerfully and consciously determining your life through the law of attraction. It's that easy. But then the most obvious question becomes, why isn't everybody living the life of their dreams? It's simply because they are thinking more about what they don't want than what they do want. Listen to your thoughts, and listen to the words you are saying. The law is absolute and there are no mistakes.

The "Don't Want" Recession

An economic recession worse than any stock market crash the world has ever seen has been raging for centuries. It is the "don't want" recession. People keep this recession alive when they predominantly think, speak, act, and focus on what they "don't want." But this is the generation that will change history, because we are receiving the knowledge that can free us! It begins with you, and you can become a pioneer of this new thought movement by simply thinking and speaking about what you do want.

When you focus your thoughts on something you don't want, and you hold that focus, you are in that moment summoning it with the mightiest power in the Universe. The law of attraction doesn't compute "don't" or "not" or "no," or any other words of negation. As you speak words of negation, the law of attraction receives a very different request.

For instance, when you say, "I don't want to lose my clients."

The law of attraction hears, *I want to lose my clients.*

When you say, "I don't want to lose my job."

The law of attraction hears, *I want to lose my job.*

When you say, "I don't want any more bills right now."

The law of attraction hears, *I want more bills right now.*

When you say, "I don't want my business to fail."

The law of attraction hears, *"I want my business to fail."*

When you say, "I don't want to lose all my money."

The law of attraction hears, *"I want to lose my money."*

When you say, "I don't want to be audited."

The law of attraction hears, *"I want to be audited."*

The law of attraction is giving you what you are thinking about—period!

You might be surprised to find just how literal the law of attraction can be.

One young couple shared a strong desire for something they wanted more than anything else in the world—a home of their own.

However, the wife was even more adamant about what she didn't want—a square house. Of course, we all have our preferences and our own sense of style, and this woman had a particularly strong aversion to modernist, glass box-style architecture. Well, the Universe conspired to deliver to this couple the most amazing opportunity to buy their first home—the kind of deal you just can't refuse. The house was perfect in every single way, except for one—it was a modernist, glass box-style house. The lesson being: when you focus on what you don't want, the Universe delivers what you don't want.

Whatever the financial situation you are currently in, it is one that you have brought into reality through your thoughts. If it is not what you want, then you have created it unconsciously, but still you created it. When you can see this, you will understand how powerful you are at creating. And now all you have to do is create what you want, consciously!

To attract money, you must consciously focus on wealth.

Never Say, "I Can't Afford It!"

As I mentioned earlier, often when people think about things they like, they will then sabotage themselves by thinking, "I can't afford that!" or "I don't have enough money for that!"

It is impossible to bring more money into your life when you are noticing you do not have enough, because that means you are thinking *thoughts* that you do not have enough. Focus on not enough money, and you will create untold more circumstances of not having enough money. To attract more money, you must focus on an abundance of money to bring that to you. You can't bring more of anything into your life by focusing on its lack.

If the words "I can't afford it" have passed your lips, your power to change that is *now*. Change it with "I can afford that! I can buy that!" Say it over and over. Become like a parrot. For the next thirty days, make it your intention that you are going to look at everything you like and say to yourself, "I can afford that. I can buy that." As you see your dream car drive past, say, "I can afford that." As you see clothes you love, as you think about a great vacation, say, "I can afford that." As you do this, you will begin to shift yourself and you will begin to *feel* better about money. You will begin to convince yourself that you can afford those things, and as you do, the pictures of your life will change.

You have to emit a new signal with your thoughts, and those thoughts should be that you currently have more than enough. You really do need to call your imagination into play and make believe you already have the money you want. And it is so much fun to do! You will notice as you pretend and play games of having wealth that you feel instantly better about money, and as you feel better about it, it will begin to flow into your life.

If you believe you have been focusing on an abundance of money and yet no money has appeared, that does not mean the law of attraction is not working. You cannot ever say the law of attraction is not working, because it is working all the time. Each of us is attracting in every moment of our lives. If you don't have what you want, you are seeing the effect of your use of the law. If you don't have what you want, and you are observing *not having* what you want and thinking about *not having* what you want, then you are creating *not having* what you want. You are either attracting what you want or you are attracting the absence of what you want. You are still creating and the law is still responding to you. And that is because the law is exact, the law is precise, and it never fails. When it appears that it isn't working, you can be guaranteed it is not the law that is failing. When things are not appearing as wanted, it is always because the person is not using the law correctly.

This is great news! Didn't it take practice to walk?
Didn't it take practice to drive?

Practice is all that stands between you and a life of
abundance and prosperity!

How Long Does It Take?

As you stay focused on what you want instead of
observing *not having* what you want, it's common
to ask, "How long does it take for the cash to
arrive?"

There is no time for the Universe just as there is no
size for the Universe. It is as easy to manifest one
dollar as it is to manifest one million dollars. It is
the same process, and the only reason why one
may come faster and the other may take longer
is because you thought that a million dollars was
a lot of money and that one dollar was not very
much.

When you think something is really big, in effect
you're saying to the law of attraction, "This is so
big it's going to be difficult to achieve, and it's
probably going to take a really long time." And
you will be right, because whatever you think is
what you will receive. If you think your desire

is really big, you will create difficulty and a time delay in receiving what you want. But there is no big or small for the Universe, and there is no concept of time for the Universe.

To help you have the true perspective of creation, no matter how big your desire may seem to you, think of it as the size of a dot! You may want a house, car, vacation, a million dollars . . . It doesn't matter what it is you want, think of it as the size of a dot, because for the Universe, what you want is smaller than a dot!

Start With Something Small

To help get you started on your law-of-attraction journey, try attracting something small like a cup of coffee. Most people can manifest the small things quickly. This is because they do not have as much resistance around their ability to attract the small things, and because they're less likely to think contradictory thoughts.

For one man, attracting something small rather quickly became a matter of necessity as well as pride. He had just arrived home from work when his wife told him they had no money for food and would need to borrow $20 from her mother to last *them until payday. On a whim, he told her not to worry as he had $20 that he had left at work. This was a white lie—there was no $20 at work, at least that he was aware of. He applied the law of attraction, picturing the $20 as he went to bed that night. Just to be certain that it was his $20, he imagined it with the number 500 written across it in blue pen.*

The next day, he went in to work confident in the fact that his $20 would be delivered to him, one way or another. Around lunchtime, the manager of HR came down to see him to let him know that he had won $20 as second prize in the work lottery. When he was handed his prize, sure enough, the number 500 was scrawled across it in blue.

If your desire is to attract money, then you could start by attracting a marked $20 bill like this man did. Or you could make it a silver dollar or a gold coin or a brand-new, shiny quarter. Anything specific to your currency will do, but make sure it's a little bit special so you'll know when you've attracted it, like choosing a coin from a particular year. Focus on that shiny coin, but don't concern yourself with how it's going to come to you. It could be given to you in change, or you might find it in your pocket, or behind the cushions on your sofa, or you might stumble across it on the sidewalk. It really doesn't matter how the shiny coin comes to you, when you focus on the coin the Universe moves people, circumstances, and events to deliver that coin to you.

Starting with something small, like a shiny coin, is an easy way to experience the law of attraction in action. As you experience the power you have to attract, you will move on to creating much bigger things.

If the bigger things you desire include substantial amounts of money, then just like the shiny coin, you need not concern yourself with how the money comes to you. If you held thoughts in the past that the only way money could come to you was through your job, then let those go immediately. Can you appreciate that as you continue to think that, it must be your experience? Such thoughts do not serve you. So don't limit the ways in which money can come to you. Instead, focus your predominant thoughts on wealth, give no thoughts to lack or scarcity, and you will be well on your way to prosperity.

LESSON 2

FEELINGS ABOUT MONEY

You create your life with your thoughts.
Because you are always thinking, you are always
creating, and so what you think about the most or
focus on the most is what will appear as your life.

That means that your life right now is a reflection of
your *past* thoughts. Think of all the good things in
your life. And now realize that you brought them all
into your life. Your thoughts moved the energies of
the Universe to bring all those good things to you.

Obviously, the reverse is also true. All the things
that people consider to be not so good in their
life—like increasing debt, unpaid bills, or not

having enough money to pay the rent—were attracted by their thoughts.

Now I know how that sounds, and most certainly we all know that no one would ever deliberately attract anything unwanted, especially not struggles with money. But without the knowledge of The Secret, it is easy to see how some unwanted things may have occurred in your life or other people's lives. They simply came from a lack of awareness of the great creative power of thought.

The point is, your life is in your hands. No matter where you are now, no matter what has happened in the past, you can begin to consciously choose your thoughts, and you can change your life.

For anyone struggling under a mountain of debt, this may well be the best news they've heard in a long time—by consciously choosing *only positive* thoughts about money, you can overcome any financial difficulties. Remember, nothing can come into your experience unless you summon it through persistent thoughts.

However, scientific research has established that you have around sixty thousand thoughts every day. With so many thoughts a day, how can you even tell when your thoughts are positive and when they are negative?

Through your feelings! Your feelings tell you very quickly what you're thinking. Whenever you think about what you want and love, you feel good.

But of course, the reverse is also true. Think back to a time when your feelings suddenly took a dive—maybe when you were hit with a very large bill that you couldn't afford to pay. That feeling in your stomach or solar plexus was instant. Those feelings are an immediate signal for you to know that your thoughts are negative.

So you want to become aware of how you're feeling, and get in tune with how you're feeling, because it is the fastest way for you to know what you're thinking. And when you know what you're thinking, then you'll know what you are in the process of attracting.

Feel Good About Money

If you feel good when you think about money, then you will receive back positive circumstances and experiences surrounding money. But if you feel bad when you think about money, perhaps because you don't have enough, then you must receive back negative circumstances and experiences of not having enough money. Those negative feelings you're experiencing are a sure sign of your negative thinking about money, and they forecast what you are in the process of attracting.

For one young woman, outstanding repair bills for her car forced her into working three dead-end jobs that made her feel frustrated and miserable. No matter how hard she worked, she never seemed to have enough money to clear her debts. Finally, she managed to scrape together enough cash and was on her way to make the final payment for the repairs, when she sustained even more damage to her car. This plunged her further into debt, resulting in even more negative thoughts and negative feelings. Instinctively, she knew the only way out of this cycle of negativity was to begin to think better thoughts and feel good. She decided to quit two of her jobs and dip into her savings to cover the bills while she worked on feeling better.

A short time later, a job opportunity came up working as a chef in a retail establishment. The more she looked into it, the more she came to see that this was her dream job, and that she was perfectly qualified. However, she faced a competitive field of applicants and had to go through several rounds of interviews and a full presentation in front of company heads. But with her fresh, positive outlook and good feelings

*about herself, she was able to rise above all the
other candidates to secure the position. She was
delighted to find that her starting wage was
significantly higher than she'd expected, and she
was able to clear all of her debts quickly. She can
now afford to live the life she always wanted, and
all thanks to her focus on feeling good regardless
of her circumstances.*

The most important thing for you to know is that
your good feelings are always associated with
good thoughts and your bad feelings are always
associated with bad thoughts. It is impossible
to feel bad and at the same time be having good
thoughts. That would defy the law, because
your thoughts cause your feelings. If you are
feeling anxious over the state of your finances,
it is because you are thinking thoughts that are
making you feel anxious.

As you feel anxious about money, and don't make
any effort to change your thoughts and feel better,
you are in effect saying, "Bring me more financial
circumstances that will make me feel anxious.
Bring it on!"

Likewise, it is impossible to feel good about
money and at the same time be having negative
thoughts. If you are feeling good, it is because you
are thinking good thoughts.

As you are thinking good thoughts, you are emitting a powerful frequency that is attracting back to you more good things that will make you feel good. Be aware that as you are feeling good, you are powerfully attracting *all* good things to you—including money.

A Shortcut to Riches

I want to let you in on a secret to The Secret. The shortcut to anything you want in your life is to *be* and *feel* happy NOW! It is the fastest way to bring money and anything else you want into your life. Focus on radiating out into the Universe those feelings of joy and happiness. When you do that, you are inevitably thinking thoughts of joy and happiness, and you will attract back to you all things that bring you joy and happiness. This will not only include an abundance of money, but everything else you are wanting. The law of attraction is reflecting back your innermost thoughts and feelings as the pictures and experiences of your life.

Simply put, feeling happy now is the fastest way to bring money and anything else you like into your life.

If you are like most people, you have been living your life saying to yourself, "I will be happy when we have more money," or "I will be happy when I have a better house," or "I will be happy when I get a job or promotion," or "I will be happy when the kids are through college," or "I will be happy when I can travel." If that's the case, you will never have those things, because your thoughts are defying the law of attraction.

You have to be happy first to receive happy things! It can't happen any other way, because whatever you want to receive in life, you must first radiate out through your thoughts and feelings! You cannot control *all* of your thoughts, but you are in command of your feelings, and you can change the way you feel about any situation, no matter what is happening around you.

When you change the way you feel about a situation, the situation must change to mirror your new thoughts and feelings. If something negative has happened in your life, you can change the situation by changing the way you feel. It is never too late, because you can always change the way you feel. To receive what you desire, to change anything into what you desire, no matter what the subject, all it takes is changing the way you feel!

You may want to travel, but if you feel disappointment because you can't travel, then on the subject of travel, you will continue to receive disappointing circumstances in which you cannot travel, until you change the way you feel. The law of attraction will move every circumstance for you to travel, but you have to *feel good* about travel to receive it.

Money is no different. You have got to *feel good* about money to attract more to you.

How do you feel about money?

Most people would say they feel good about money, but if they don't have enough, they don't feel good about it at all. If a person has all the money they need, then most certainly they feel good about money. So you can tell how you feel about money, because if you don't have all you need, then you don't feel good about money. This is important because the money in your life will never change while you don't feel good about it. In fact, those negative feelings about money are stopping more money coming to you! And worse still, those negative feelings about money attract negative circumstances such as big bills or things breaking down, which are all circumstances that drain you of money. When you react with negative feelings to a big bill, you give out more negative feelings about money, which bring even more negative circumstances to you that drain you of more money.

You have got to stop the cycle, and you stop it by starting to feel good about money. When you change the way you feel about money, the amount of money in your life will change. The better you feel about money, the more money you magnetize to yourself.

A Game to Feel Good About Money

Here is a game you can play so you remember to feel good about money each time you handle it. Imagine a dollar bill. Imagine the front of the dollar bill as the positive side, which represents plenty of money. Imagine the back of the dollar bill as the negative side representing a lack of money. Each time you handle money, deliberately flip the bills so the front is facing you. Put bills in your wallet with the front facing you. When you hand over money, make sure the front is facing upward. By doing this you are using money as your cue to remember to feel good about plenty of money.

Seize every moment that you are handling money to make the money multiply by feeling good. Feel good when you pay for anything! Feel good when you hand over money! Feel good about what you are paying for and don't resent the fact that you now have less money. Feel good about everything that money brings into your life. Feel good for the groceries. Feel good for the clothes you wear. Feel good for the gasoline and feel good for the car you drive. Feel good for the home you live in. Feel good for the electricity and the telephone and water supply.

Always remember that you are receiving valuable goods and services in exchange for your money and that is something to feel good about.

As you feel good for things you are buying, it will make you feel good about the money you're giving instead of feeling bad because you have less money.

Ways to Feel Good About Bills

If you don't have much money, then it's probably true that receiving bills won't make you feel good. But the moment you react negatively to a big bill, those bad feelings ensure that you will continue to attract more bills. The most important thing is that when you pay your bills, you find a way, any way, to make yourself feel good. Never pay your bills when you don't feel good, because you will just bring bigger bills to you. You have to find a way that works for you to focus on prosperity, *despite* the bills around you. You have to find a way of feeling good, so you can bring your good to you.

To change what you're feeling, you need to use your imagination to turn your bills into something that makes you feel better. You can imagine they're not really bills at all but instead you've decided to donate money to each company or person out of the goodness of your heart, because of the wonderful service they provide.

A game I created that helped shift my feelings about my pile of bills was to pretend that the bills were actually checks. As I opened them, I would jump for joy and say, "More money for me! Thank you. Thank you." I took each bill, imagined it was a check, and then I added a zero to it in my mind to make it even more. I got a notepad and wrote at the top of the page "I have received," and then I would list all the amounts of the bills with an added zero. Next to each amount I would write "Thank you," and feel the feelings of gratitude for receiving it—to the point where I had tears in my eyes. Then I would take each bill, which looked very small compared to what I had imagined receiving, and I paid it in my mind with gratitude until I literally received enough funds to be able to pay it.

I never opened my bills until I had got myself into the feeling that they were checks. If I opened my bills before convincing myself they were checks, my stomach would churn when I opened them. I knew that the emotion of the churning in my stomach was powerfully bringing more bills. I knew I had to erase that feeling, that fear, and replace it with joyful feelings, so I could bring more money into my life. In the face of a pile of bills, that game worked for me, and it changed my life.

Naturally, I would have loved to have known about this much earlier in life, and so it's always a delight to hear about young people using The Secret to overcome their own struggles with money.

For a recent college graduate, the stress of covering his monthly student-loan repayments was becoming a regular source of anxiety. Raising the $494 each month was hard enough at the best of times, but when his regular work dried up, he had no idea how he was going to pay. That's when he decided to apply the law of attraction and hopefully end this cycle of money worries that he felt each month. Instead of stressing over where *he would get the money, he made the effort to shift his energy from negative to positive. And anytime a thought arose about the payment, he simply pictured a friendly, smiling face handing him exactly $494.*

Shortly after, he was offered a one-off gig as a bouncer at a bar over a holiday weekend. The job didn't pay very well, and it promised to be hard work and long hours controlling a raucous holiday crowd. But with nothing better on offer, he took the job. Come the weekend, he was surprised how much he enjoyed himself. In fact, it didn't even feel like work to him as he met many new friends and had a great time.

At the end of the weekend, after closing time, the bar staff gathered to enjoy a quiet drink together. That's when the bar manager approached him, smiling and handing over an envelope containing his share of the weekend's tips. Better still, he offered regular work through the rest of the summer. The college graduate happily accepted. Later, as he counted out his share of the tips, he was amazed to find $494 — he had manifested the exact amount of money he needed, and it arrived in exactly the same way he had imagined — with a happy, smiling face handing it to him. And all because he shifted the way he felt from worry over money to feeling good.

Fear and the Law of Attraction

If you have feelings about money that involve
worry or even fear, then of course, you cannot
receive more money. The law of attraction says
that like attracts like, so if you feel fearful about
the state of your money, then you must receive
more situations that will continue to make you
fearful about money.

Fear is one of the most debilitating emotions that
there is, but the truth is, every one of us can live
a life without fear. The key to absolute freedom
and joy for each and every one of us is to let go of
fear. When you understand that fear puts you on
a frequency of attracting more fearful events and
circumstances into your life, you will understand
how important it is to shift yourself. People are
in fear of losing their job, of not being able to pay
the bills, of foreclosure on their mortgage, and the
list goes on. But the fear of those things is actually
summoning them to us. The law of attraction
is impersonal, and whatever we focus on with
feeling is coming to us.

A perfect example to demonstrate fear and the
law of attraction in action is this: you may know
of people who acquired massive wealth, lost it all,
and within a short time acquired massive wealth

again. What happened in these cases, whether they knew it or not, was that their dominant thoughts were on wealth; that is how they acquired it in the first instance. Then they allowed fearful thoughts of losing the wealth to enter their minds, until those fearful thoughts of loss became their dominant thoughts. They tipped the scales from thinking thoughts of wealth to thinking thoughts of loss, and so they lost it all. Once they had lost it, however, the fear of loss disappeared, and they tipped the scales back with dominant thoughts of wealth. And wealth returned.

The law responds to your thoughts, no matter what they may be. When fearful thoughts come, stamp them out immediately. Send them on their way and replace them with anything that makes you feel good.

According to The Secret, you can have, be, or do whatever you want in your life, no limits. But there's one catch: you have to feel good. And when you think about it, isn't that all you ever want? The law of attraction is indeed perfect.

LESSON 3

A WEALTH MINDSET

Now that you know The Secret, when you see someone who is wealthy you will know that that person's predominant thoughts are on wealth and not on lack. They have drawn wealth to them through the law of attraction—whether they did it consciously or unconsciously. They focused on thoughts of wealth, and the Universe moved people, circumstances, and events to deliver wealth to them. The wealth that they have, you can have also. The only difference between you and them is that they thought the thoughts to bring the wealth to them. Your wealth is waiting for you in the invisible, so to bring it into the visible, think wealth!

However, attracting wealth through the law of attraction doesn't necessarily mean that you will hold on to that wealth. That's because making wealth stick to you requires consistency with your thoughts. It's the difference between thinking about money only when you need money, and changing your whole relationship with money so that you change your way of life.

What do I mean by that?

Okay, well imagine that you are wealthy right now. Imagine that you have all the money you need right now. How would you live your life differently? Think about all the things you would do. How would you feel? You would feel different, and because you would feel different, you would walk differently. You would talk differently. You would hold your body in a different way, and you would move differently. You would react differently to everything. Your reaction to bills would be different. Your reaction to people, circumstances, events, and everything in life would be different. Because you would *feel* different! You would be relaxed. You would have peace of mind. You would feel happy. You would be easygoing about everything. You would enjoy every day, without giving any concern to tomorrow.

The reason that you would walk differently and talk differently and feel differently and live differently is that you would be fundamentally different.

The difference between someone who is struggling financially and someone who has a fabulous life of wealth comes down to one thing— it's their *mindset*.

Wealth Mindset vs. Poverty Mindset

People who are happy and successful think more about the good things that can happen, think more about having happiness, having money, and creating a rich and meaningful life, than they do the opposite of those things. They have a *wealth* mindset.

People who are struggling are unintentionally using their imagination for what they don't want, and are feeling the negativity of what they're imagining. They are often overwhelmed by thoughts and fears of lack and struggle. They have a *poverty* mindset.

A mindset is such a simple thing, but it creates vast differences in people's lives.

It explains why the top few percent own the vast majority of the world's wealth. These people not only attracted money to themselves, but they also made money stick to themselves. If you took all the money in the world and you distributed it equally to every person, within a short time all the money would be back in the hands of the few percent. This is because the law of attraction responds to a wealth mindset, and so the few percent with a wealth mindset would magnetize the money back to them. The law of attraction moves all the money and riches in the world, and it moves it toward a wealth mindset.

You can see the law of attraction and mindsets working together when people win the lottery. These winners imagined and felt with all their heart that they would win the lottery. They spoke about *when* they win the lottery, not *if* they win the lottery, and they planned and imagined what they would do *when* they won. They believed they would win and they won! But the statistics on lottery winners show the real evidence of having a wealth or a poverty mindset. Within a few years of winning, the majority of people have lost the money and are in more debt than before the lottery.

This happens because they used the law of attraction to win the lottery, but even when they received money, they didn't change their mindset about money, and they lost it all. The money didn't stick to them!

When you have a poverty mindset, you repel money. It will never stick to you. Even when you get some extra money you hadn't figured on receiving, in no time at all you will find that it has slipped through your fingers. Bigger bills come in, things break down, and unforeseen circumstances of every kind occur, all of which drains you of money and takes it right out of your hands.

So why is it that so many people have a poverty mindset? It's not just because they have never had money, as many of the wealthiest people on the planet began with nothing. The reason why so many people have a poverty mindset is that they retain negative beliefs about money, and those negative beliefs were fed into their subconscious minds when they were children. Beliefs like "We can't afford that," "Money is evil," "Rich people must be dishonest," "Wanting money is wrong and it's not spiritual," "Having plenty of money means hard work."

When you're a child, you accept just about everything told to you by your parents, teachers, or society. And so without realizing it, if you're like most people, you grew up having a negative mindset about money. The irony is that at the same time that you're told that wanting money is wrong, you are told that you have to earn a living, even if it means doing work you don't love. Maybe you were even told that there are only certain jobs you can do to earn a living—that it's a limited list.

None of these things is true. The people who told you these things are innocent because they were passing on what they believed and felt was true, but because they believed it, the law of attraction made it true in their lives.

This was very much the life experience for one young man from a working-class family, who had dreams of becoming a creative writer. Despite excelling at school, he was raised to believe that the best opportunities were reserved for the wealthy and the well connected. So he left school and went to work in a factory, where he stayed for nine long years, working on a production line. He hated the work, and his colleagues were generally angry and unpleasant. In the meantime, he applied for many different jobs requiring creative talent, but was always told he lacked qualifications or experience. He looked into further education, but being surrounded by so much negativity about money, he convinced himself that he could never afford the tuition fees. This, of course, became a self-fulfilling prophecy—the courses that appealed to him were all way too expensive.

It was only when he discovered The Secret that he began to develop a more positive outlook and belief in himself. He convinced himself to take satisfaction from his work each day, and to appreciate his job and the people he worked with. Then each night, as he went to bed, he imagined receiving a call from a new employer offering him his dream job. He would drift off to sleep crying tears of joy.

Soon after, a friend alerted him to a local radio station seeking a copywriter for their advertisements. He applied immediately, and was invited to submit sample scripts for an advertising campaign. As he worked on the assignment, he imagined he was doing the job for real, and it felt so right. Suddenly, his aspirations of being a creative writer went from being no more than a pipe dream to something he truly believed in. He swept through the interview process without anyone asking about his qualifications or experience—they were simply so impressed by his talent and positive self-belief that it didn't seem to matter. He was offered the job in a phone call, just as he had imagined. He had risen from a dead-end factory job to become a creative writer at a radio station simply by changing his mindset about what he could do.

If you lack money in your life, or opportunities in your career, it is because you are thinking more negative thoughts than you are thinking positive thoughts. That in essence is a poverty mindset.

I came from a working-class family, and even though my parents didn't desire a lot of money, they struggled to make ends meet. So I grew up with the same negative beliefs about money as most people. I grew up with a poverty mindset. I knew I had to change my mindset about money to change my circumstances. I knew I had to change myself completely so money would not only come to me but stick to me!

Like every other human being, one of the most difficult things for me to wrestle with was my mindset. But once I really got it that I was thwarting my own success and making myself miserable, that's when I began to adopt a positive mindset—about money and everything else in life. And I did that with one positive thought at a time.

You see, your mindset is of your own creation. It's your *beliefs* that form your mindset, and all beliefs are simply repeated thoughts with strong feelings attached to them. Therefore, the first step in changing your mindset is to take responsibility for your own thoughts. Once you accept that it's the thoughts you are thinking that attract riches or keep you in poverty, then you will begin to change the kinds of thoughts you think. And as you do that, you will choose to start looking at life through optimistic eyes.

Choose Optimism

The truth is, every single person with a wealth mindset is an optimist when it comes to money. You have the freedom to *choose* to be optimistic or pessimistic—about money and everything else in your life. You can choose to peel off your old, negative mindset like a suit of clothes, and put on a brand-spanking-new mindset every single day by changing your thoughts about money. It's as simple as that.

Now, some might argue that it's not so simple to choose to be positive or optimistic under the weight of extremely negative circumstances—

for instance, unemployment, homelessness, bankruptcy, or any other misfortune.

However, as the experience of one struggling businessman shows, there is no such thing as a hopeless situation—every single circumstance of your life can change.

In this man's case he had taken over a family business, but lacking experience and support, he ran it into the ground and was forced to close the doors. On the brink of bankruptcy, he carried $100,000 in personal debt, and was working three jobs just trying to make ends meet. He was exhausted and stressed, with his new marriage on the rocks, and wondering how it all got so bad. He made a desperate decision to take his own life, but at the last instant, he changed his mind. That very day his mother introduced him to The Secret documentary film, and as he watched it, tears streamed down his cheeks. He realized that all of the negative circumstances were of his own making due to his negative thinking. It then occurred to him that if he was capable of creating so much misfortune, then he was equally capable of creating a fortune. His entire outlook on life was transformed.

Soon after, he entered real estate sales, and set himself a goal of earning $100,000 in a year—the *same amount as his debt. He achieved that goal with ease, and has since gone on to live a life of prosperity and abundance, bringing in over a million dollars a year, thanks to his newfound self-belief and a positive outlook.*

Because of the duality on Earth, there are always going to be both positive and negative experiences. But if you consistently look for the good and maintain a positive attitude despite outside circumstances, you will triumph.

On the other hand, if you look to outside circumstances in the world to form your attitude, you'll be in trouble. That would require every circumstance around you to be perfect all the time so you could be positive, and you cannot control every circumstance. It would also require a lot of people to behave perfectly all the time, and you cannot control anyone but yourself. If you think about it, you would actually need all the billions of us to shape up into what you want so you can have a positive attitude. You simply can't look to outside circumstances to dictate what kind of attitude you will have. If you do, you will always find a circumstance or a person that will give you a reason to have a negative attitude. In order to become your most powerful tool, your attitude must be dictated from *within*.

To establish a positive attitude, it doesn't matter what financial state you are in now. It doesn't even matter what financial state your business, your country, or the world is in. In fact, there are people who lived during the Great Depression who thrived because they maintained their wealth mindset. They remained positive and optimistic, and they defied the circumstances and the air of extreme pessimism that surrounded them.

A positive and optimistic attitude doesn't mean you don't have occasional down days. You *will* have some down days. It's not about the occasional down days, though; it's about how many of the precious days of your life you're enjoying because of your positive and optimistic attitude.

I'm sure you've known someone who is always up and has a cheerful and bright attitude or outlook toward life, and when you are with them you also feel fantastic and full of life. That's what an optimistic attitude does to you.

On the other hand, a pessimistic attitude toward life means a miserable life. At some point in your life you've no doubt encountered someone who is pessimistic about everything, and when you are with them it sucks the energy and the joy out of you. Well, that's precisely what a pessimistic outlook or attitude does to you.

A pessimist is never happy. It's not possible, because even if they had everything they wanted, the glass would still look half-empty to them! That's why a pessimist can never have what they want. And that's why you must do everything you can to be an optimist rather than a pessimist.

So how do you flip from being a pessimist to being an optimist? How do you change your poverty mindset into a wealth mindset regardless of what is happening around you?

Well, there are a few positive traits of optimistic people that you can adopt to help form your wealth mindset and to live the life of your dreams.

Don't Discuss Bad News

The first thing to do is to avoid talking about any difficulties with money, a failed deal, or that the profits of your business are down. Stop talking about a bad event in the news, or a person or situation that annoyed or frustrated you. Don't talk about the bad day you had, being late for an appointment, getting caught in traffic, or missing the bus. There are many little things that happen each day; if you get caught up in talking about the negative things that happen, then every one of those little things brings more struggle and difficulty to your life.

Instead, you have to talk about the good news of the day. Talk about the appointment that went well. Talk about how you love being on time. Talk about how good it is to be full of health. Talk about the profits you want your business to achieve. Talk about the situations and interactions you had in your day that went well. You have to talk about the good things, to bring all good things to you.

If someone offered you the life of your dreams in exchange for you finding many good things to talk about, you would do it in a flash. Well, that is the way you receive the life of your dreams!

Don't Complain

Another positive trait among optimists that you should adopt is the refusal to complain or be discouraged when things don't go your way.

Just ask yourself whether you think complaining can transform a person's life into success and happiness. Do you think being easily discouraged or dejected by bad news can fulfill a person's dreams and give them financial freedom?

Complaining and being dejected are excuses we make when we're not living the life we came here to live. And because we see people around us who complain and get discouraged, we can get the mistaken impression that it's okay and won't harm us. But all of those negative emotions will pull you down and disempower you until you feel hopeless. None of those emotions can ever fill you with the happiness and success you want and deserve. None of those emotions will lead you to the life of your dreams.

For a college student attending an expensive private university, the announcement of cuts to her financial-aid package could easily have sent her spiraling into negativity. She learned that she would only receive around $5,000, and would therefore be short by up to $35,000 to cover her tuition for the following year. Many of her fellow students had received similar cuts to their award packages and had taken to social media in fury, claiming that their education was over. But rather than join them in their blaming and complaining, this young woman chose to remain positive. She was grateful for her education, refusing to

*criticize the university, and felt optimistic that
somehow, it would all work out in her favor.
She prayed and thanked God, the Universe, and
anyone else in advance for helping pay for her
tuition fees. She researched available scholarships
and grants, and inquired at the financial-aid office
about having her case reviewed. She was invited
to fill out an application online, and so she went
back to double-check the amount of her award and
exactly how much she was short. When she did,
she was amazed to find that the final award figure
had already changed—now there was no shortfall,
and she was being completely covered for her
tuition fees for the following year. As this young
woman discovered, it pays to stay positive.*

Desire Everything, Need Nothing

One last trait of a wealth mindset that you should
look to adopt is to *desire* everything and *need*
nothing.

To desire something is in proper accordance with
the law of attraction. You attract what you desire.
To need something is misuse of the law. You
cannot attract what you *need* if you feel you need
it urgently or desperately, because that emotion

contains fear. That kind of "needing" keeps things away.

When you *need* money, it is a powerful feeling within you; it comes from the thought that you don't have enough money, and of course through the law of attraction you continue to create not having enough money.

I can speak from experience about *needing* money, because just before I discovered The Secret my accountants told me that my company had suffered a major loss that year, and in three months it would be history. After ten years of hard work, my company was about to slip through my fingers. And as I *needed* more money to save my company, things just got worse. There seemed no way out.

Then I discovered The Secret, and everything in my life—including the state of my company—was totally transformed, because I changed the way I was thinking. As my accountants continued to fuss about the figures and focus on that, I kept my mind focused on abundance and all being well. I *knew* with every fiber of my being that the Universe would provide, and it did. It provided in ways I could not have imagined. I had my moments of doubt, but when the doubt came, I immediately moved my thoughts to the outcome of what I desired.

If you have "needing money" in your frequency, then you will keep attracting "needing money." You have to find a way to focus on abundance despite the outside circumstances, because it is when you no longer feel the *need* for money that money will come.

Lesson 4

The Creative Process for Money

According to the law of attraction, what you are thinking now is creating your future life. Since you attract to you what you think about most, it is easy to see what your dominant thoughts have been on the subject of money, because that is your experience. That's to say, the contents of your wallet, your bank balance, and the entire state of your finances are all due to the thoughts you have been thinking. But that was in the past.

Now you are learning The Secret, and with this knowledge, you can radically change the circumstances of money in your life simply by changing the way you think. You are a creator, and there is an easy process for you to follow to create your own wealth and attract anything you want through the law of attraction.

This Creative Process has three simple steps—Ask, Believe, and Receive.

Step 1: ASK

You get to choose what you want, but you must get clear about it. And when it comes to money, you must get clear on exactly how much you want. If you're not clear, then the law of attraction cannot bring you what you want. You will be sending out a mixed frequency, and you can only attract mixed results. Perhaps for the first time in your life, work out what it is you really want. Now that you know you can have, be, or do anything, and there are no limits, ask yourself, "How much money do I want, and exactly what do I want my life to be like?"

This can be a lot of fun. It really is like having the Universe as your own personal ATM. You might think to yourself, "I'd like to live in this particular city, I'd like to drive that car, I'd like to vacation at a certain tropical resort, and I'd like to have this much money in the bank."

To help you get clear about what you *really* want, sit down with your phone, computer, or pen and paper and make a list of all the things you want in every area of your life. Think through every detail of what you want to be, do, or have.

If you want money to educate your children, work out the details of their education, including which school you want your children to attend, the cost of the school fees, books, food, clothing, and transportation, so that you know exactly how much money you will need.

If you want to travel, then write down the details of the countries you want to visit, how long you want to travel for, what you want to see and do, where you want to stay, and how much spending money you'll require.

Whatever you desire, tally up the cost in dollars, so you can make a withdrawal from the Bank of the Universe. It really is as simple as that.

Bear in mind that wealth comes in many forms and money is just one of those forms. So, other than asking specifically for money, you can simply ask for what you want to do or have or be. Don't limit your life by thinking money is the only way to get something you want. If you want a new home, you just need to ask. If you want beautiful clothes, appliances, or a brand-new car, just ask! All these things can come to you in an unlimited number of ways besides money.

In fact, I know of people who have used this process to attract overseas holidays, luxury cruises, new cars, college tuition, and much more without spending a cent. It all comes down to focusing on what you want and allowing the Universe to use its infinite ways to make it happen. And when you get clear in your mind about exactly what it is you want, you have completed the first step in the Creative Process: you have asked.

Step 2: BELIEVE

You must believe that you have received. You must know that the money, or whatever it is you want, is yours the moment you ask. You must have complete and utter faith. If you had requested a withdrawal at a bank, you would relax, knowing you were going to receive the exact amount you requested, and you would get on with your life.

In the moment you ask, and believe and know you already have the money in the unseen, the entire Universe shifts to bring it into the seen. You must act, speak, and think as though you are receiving it now. Why? The Universe is a mirror, and the law of attraction is mirroring back to you your dominant thoughts. So doesn't it make sense that you have to see yourself as receiving the money? If your thoughts contain noticing you do not have it yet, you will continue to attract not having it yet. You must believe you have it already. You must believe you have received it. You have to emit the feeling frequency of having received it, to bring those pictures back as your life.

As an example, if you win money in a lottery, even before you physically receive the money, you know it is yours. As you hold the winning ticket, that is the feeling of believing the money is yours. That is the feeling of believing you have it already. That is the feeling of believing you have received. Claim the things you want by feeling and believing they are yours already. When you do that, the law of attraction will powerfully move all circumstances, people, and events for you to receive.

Of course, you can attract any amount of money you want, but to do that you must follow the principles of the law of attraction—you must believe and you must eliminate doubt. Understand that when you allow a thought of doubt to enter your mind, the law of attraction will soon line up one doubtful thought after another. Obviously, the law of attraction cannot give you what you want when your predominant thoughts are of doubt. Therefore, you must eliminate doubt and replace it with the full expectation that you will receive what you are asking for. If you are not receiving what you are asking for, it is not the law that has failed. It means that your doubt has overridden your belief. This is because the law of attraction is responding to your predominant thoughts *all the time*, not just in the moment you ask. That's why after you've asked, you must continue to believe and know. Have faith. Your belief that you *have* what you've asked for, that undying faith, is your greatest power. When you believe you are receiving, get ready, and watch the magic begin!

Step 3: RECEIVE

In order to receive, you simply have to feel good now. Feel the way you expect to feel when the money arrives. Receiving money is a good feeling, and it's no coincidence that when you are feeling good, you are on the frequency of receiving; you are on the frequency of all good things coming to you, and you will receive exactly what you have asked for. You wouldn't ask for money, or anything else for that matter, unless it was going to make you feel good in the receiving of it, would you? So feel that way now—by getting yourself on the feel-good frequency. Your goal is simply to feel as good as you possibly can right now, and keep doing that.

If you're finding that doubts are really undermining your belief that you are receiving what you asked for, then there is a very powerful practice you can utilize to increase your belief.

Affirmations

Affirmations are like positive, personal mission statements which, when repeated over and over, can't help but form new beliefs. They work particularly well with money because most people have lifelong negative beliefs and doubts around money.

For instance, have you ever had the thought that you can't afford something, that you are unlucky when it comes to money, or that money seems to always slip through your fingers?

If so, then you need to replace those thoughts immediately. Say to yourself over and over, "Money sticks to me!" "I *am* lucky with money!" and "I *can* afford anything I want."

As you do, you will shift your thinking along with your beliefs, and you will begin to feel better about money.

When I was making *The Secret* documentary, with no idea where the money would come from to complete the project, I gathered a list of money affirmations to reinforce my belief. The rest, as they say, is history.

I would like to share with you some of my favorite money affirmations, which I still use most days. I recommend that you recite these affirmations to yourself daily, at least until you get to the point of believing that you are receiving what you've asked for . . .

> I am rich.
> I am a money magnet!
> I am attracting more and more money every day.
> I am becoming richer by the second.
> I love money and money loves me!
> I am grateful for everything I have.
> Money is my friend.
> Money comes to me effortlessly and easily.

I always have more money coming in than going
out.

I deserve money so I can do everything I want to
do in this life.

I attract all that I need to bring forth my success.

I am worthy of receiving money.

I am financially thriving.

I attract money easily.

I want good fortune and happiness for
everyone.

I am open to money coming to me from new
ways that I've never imagined.

I know there are unlimited ways that money can
come to me.

I am excited to see where more money is going
to come from next.

I am using money to bless my life and other
people's lives.

I have more than enough money.

I am receiving more money today.

I choose prosperity.

Every day in every way, my wealth is
increasing.

I am happy to give because my abundance is
limitless.

There is an abundance of money and it's on its
way to me.

You might also like to create your own
affirmations specific to your financial or life goals.

A college senior did exactly that as he approached graduation with no job prospects and no idea of a career path or what to do with the rest of his life. The only thing he knew for sure is that he wanted to become a multimillionaire and he wanted to retire at forty-five. And so he typed up those two intentions as his personal affirmation, and he had it laminated and placed it on his nightstand so that he could read it every morning and night.

His career progressed unremarkably, but he never lost sight of his goals thanks to his daily affirmation. Eventually, an opportunity presented itself to partner in a tech start-up, and he leapt at the chance. The company grew, steadily at first, but then a sequence of industry shake-ups resulted in dramatic expansion of their business. Suddenly, they were turning over a hundred million dollars a year. As the man met with his financial advisor to discuss the future, it occurred to him that he was approaching forty-five and his stock holdings in the company far exceeded the amount he had hoped to retire with when he was in college. He sold out to his partners soon after, having achieved his affirmation, and he is now free to spend all his time and money with his family.

The effective use of affirmations depends entirely on how much you believe them when you say them. If there is no belief, then the affirmation is just words that have no power. Belief adds power to your words. Repetition helps with belief, but more important to help you believe is feeling. So really *feel* the words in your affirmations until you truly believe what you are saying. The sooner you come to believe what you say in your words and affirmations, the sooner you will receive the life of your dreams.

How what you want will manifest, how the Universe will bring the money to you, is not your concern. Allow the Universe to do it for you. When you are trying to work out how it will happen, you are emitting a frequency that contains a lack of faith—that you don't believe you have it already. You think you have to do it and you do not believe the Universe will do it for you. The how is not your part in the Creative Process. It is your job to simply ask, to believe you are receiving, and feel happy now. Leave the details on how it will bring it about to the Universe.

So many people trip up on this and try to work out the how. They try to force the issue by taking action themselves, without realizing that these *forcing* actions are contradicting their desires. Anytime you decide to take action, you need to make sure that your actions are in tune with your desires and that they mirror what you expect to receive.

Inspired Action

Any action that is in tune with your desire is
called *inspired* action, and it differs from forcing
action in the following ways:

When you are acting in a forced way, you are in
action to try to make your desire happen. It will
feel hard and like a struggle. It will feel as if you
are trying to swim against the current of a river.

Inspired action, on the other hand, is when you
are acting to receive. Inspired action is completely
effortless, and it feels wonderful because you
are on the frequency of receiving. When you
are acting to receive, you will feel as if you are
flowing with the current of the river. It will feel
effortless. That is the feeling of inspired action,
and of being in the flow of the Universe and life.

To take inspired action, first think about what
you have asked for, and then make sure that your
actions are mirroring what you expect to receive.
Act as if you are receiving it. Do exactly what
you would do if you were receiving it today, and
take actions in your life to reflect that powerful
expectation. Make room to receive your desires,
and as you do, you are sending out that powerful
signal of expectation.

This is your chance to be creative as you use inspired actions in line with what you want. If you want a substantial amount of money, then set up your bank account so that you will be able to deposit and manage a substantial amount of money. If you want to attract a new house, then tidy up your current house so it is ready for easy packing. If you want to take an overseas trip, then get out your suitcases, update your passport, and start to plan your itinerary. Think about what you would do if you had your desire, and then take creative actions that make it clear you are receiving it now. And when your creative actions are in line with what you are asking for, you will look back and see the wonder and matrix of how the Universe brought what you wanted to you.

> *One of the best examples of using inspired action in the Creative Process comes from a young college freshman who dreamed of a life of prosperity. He wrote up a detailed list of his greatest desires, which included money, cars, a beautiful home, and his dream girl who he wanted to share it all with. He even wrote a check to himself for $10 million. He gazed upon that check every day, imagining what it would feel like to have that much money and how he would spend it. To help bring the feeling to life, he drove through affluent neighborhoods regularly, and picked out his favorite dream home. He kept an*

*image of a luxury car as the background screen
on his phone until he worked up the courage
to visit the dealership to take that car out for a
test drive. When the girl of his dreams appeared
in his life and became his girlfriend, suddenly
the life of abundance that he longed for began
to feel more real. That's when he received the
inspiration to create an app designed for college
students just like himself. It took a little time to
teach himself how to code so that he could build
that app, but once it was launched, it was an
immediate success. Within a year of release, he
was approached by a big company who offered
$10 million to buy him out—the exact amount
he had written on his check. With his newfound
wealth, he bought that home that he had driven
past so often, and then he bought his dream car,
and another one for his girlfriend. At twenty-one
years of age, he had attracted everything on his
wish list.*

Notice how this young man didn't go out of his
way to make his $10 million dream come true
through forced action. He simply focused on his
dream and allowed the inspiration to come to
him. What he did, you can do too. That's because
all knowledge, all discoveries, and all inventions
of the future are in the Universal Mind as
possibilities, waiting for the human mind to draw
them forth. There is an unlimited supply of ideas

waiting for you to tap into, and all you have to do is hold your mind on the end result.

Remember that you are like a magnet, attracting everything to you. The more you practice and begin to see the law of attraction bringing things to you, the greater your magnetizing power will be, because you will add the power of faith, belief, and knowing. And in that state, you will come to see that $10 million is a piece of cake—for the Universe, and for you.

LESSON 5

GRATITUDE FOR MONEY

Gratitude is a bridge that will take you from poverty to riches. The more grateful you can be for the money you have, even if you don't have very much, the more riches you will receive. And the more you complain about a lack of money, the poorer you will become.

If you think, "I haven't got enough money," "I can't afford to pay my bills," "My boss doesn't appreciate me," "I don't get along with my coworkers," or "My company is in financial trouble," then you must attract more of those experiences.

But if you think about what you're grateful for, like, "I love my job," "My coworkers are very supportive," "I have the best clients," "I got the biggest tax refund ever," or "I appreciate the money I have for all that it allows me to do," and you sincerely feel gratitude, the law of attraction says you must attract more of *those* things into your life.

For one woman, a new job meant a great deal more stress—so much so that there were days when she would go home crying. Then she decided to make a conscious effort to find something to be grateful for in every situation. Each morning, before she got out of her car to enter the building, she gave thanks for the day going smoothly. Every time she walked through the door to her office, she thanked God and the Universe for the dream job that she loved so much. As the weeks and months passed by, her stress levels faded away and she genuinely came to enjoy her work. But that's when news came down the line that her department was being closed. Ordinarily this would have left her devastated and angry. But she continued to be grateful as she applied for open positions elsewhere in the company. Her gratitude paid off once again. She was ultimately offered her choice of two great jobs, and she took the one that offered her a big pay raise.

Gratitude Can Change Your Life

I know of thousands of people in the worst imaginable situations who have changed their lives completely through gratitude. I have seen people who were in total poverty become wealthy through gratitude; I've seen business owners turn around failing businesses, and people who had struggled with money all their lives finally create abundance. I know of people who were chronically unemployed who went on to build successful careers. Someone I know even went from homelessness to living in a multimillion-dollar mansion and securing a dream job in no time.

And all of this occurred due to these people feeling gratitude for money, regardless of the financial situation they were in.

However difficult it may be, you have to ignore your current situation and any lack of money you may currently be experiencing, and gratitude is perhaps the easiest way for you to do that. You can't be grateful for money and disappointed about money at the same time. Nor can you be thinking grateful thoughts about money and have worried or fearful thoughts about money at the same time. When you're grateful for money, not only do you stop the negative thoughts and feelings that push money away from you, you're doing the very thing that brings more money to you! You are thinking and feeling good about money, and so by the law of attraction, you are drawing money to you.

If there's a lack of money in your life, understand that feeling worried, envious, jealous, disappointed, discouraged, doubtful, or fearful about money can never bring more money to you. That's because those feelings come from a lack of gratitude for the money you have. Complaining about money, arguing about money, getting frustrated about money, being critical of the cost of something, or making someone else feel bad about money is not an act of gratitude. When your actions are ungrateful, the money in your life can never improve; it will worsen.

No matter what your current situation, the very thought that you don't have enough money is being ungrateful for the money you have. You have to get negative thoughts about your current situation out of your mind and instead feel grateful for the money you do have, so the money in your life can increase!

Feeling grateful for money when you have very little is challenging for anyone, but when you understand that nothing will change until you're grateful, you will be inspired to do it.

The Golden Rule

Gratitude is riches and complaint is poverty; it's the golden rule of your whole life, whether in the area of your health, job, relationships, or finances.

If you find yourself in a situation where you're about to complain about something to do with money, whether it's through your words or your thoughts, ask yourself: "Am I willing to pay the price for this complaint?" Because that one complaint will slow or even stop the flow of money toward you.

Most people *think* they are grateful for money. Most people wouldn't think they complain about money more than they're grateful for money, but if there is a lack of money in their life they must be complaining without realizing it. And of course the biggest complaints come when money has to be paid out.

If you don't have enough money, paying your bills can be one of the most difficult things to do. I know, I've been there. It can seem like there is a greater stream of bills than there is money to pay them. But if you complain about your bills, then what you are really doing is complaining about money, and complaining keeps you in poverty.

It's understandable, if you don't have enough money, that the last thing you want to do is feel grateful for your bills. But that's exactly what you *have* to do to receive more money in your life. To have a rich life, you must be grateful for everything to do with money, and begrudging your bills is not being grateful. You must do the exact opposite, which is to *be grateful* for the goods or services you've *received* from those who billed you. It is such a simple thing to do, but it will have a monumental effect on the money in your life. You will literally become a money magnet!

To be grateful for a bill, think about how much you've benefitted from the service or goods on the bill. If it's payment for rent or a mortgage, be grateful that you have a home, and you're living in it. What if the only way you could live in a home was by saving up all the money and paying cash for it? What if there were no such thing as lending institutions or places to rent? Most of us would be living on the streets, so be grateful to the lending institutions or your landlord, because they have made it possible for you to live in a home or apartment.

If you're paying a bill for gas or electricity, think about the heating or cooling you received, the hot showers, and every appliance you were able to use because of the service. If you're paying a phone or internet bill, imagine how difficult your life would be if you had to travel vast distances to talk to each person individually. Think about how many times you've been able to call or text family and friends, send and receive emails, or access information instantly through the internet because of your service provider. All of these remarkable services are at your fingertips, so be grateful for them, and be grateful that the companies trust you by providing their services *before* you have paid for them.

What you will find is that feeling gratitude for the money you've paid out guarantees you will receive more. Gratitude is like a magnetic golden thread attached to your money, so when you pay money out, the money always returns to you, sometimes equally, sometimes tenfold, sometimes a hundredfold. The abundance you receive back depends not on how much money you pay, but on how much gratitude you give. You could give so much gratitude when you pay a bill for $50 that you could receive back hundreds or even thousands of dollars.

In addition to being grateful for your bills, there are a number of other ways to use the power of gratitude to attract more money into your life.

Gratitude for the Past

The first way is to be grateful for all the money and everything of value you have received throughout your life.

Think back through your childhood before you had any money of your own. Consider every instance where money was paid *for* you. For example, the food you ate, the house you lived in, your education and textbooks, vacations, birthday gifts, clothes, medical care, entertainment, transport, and all of your basic necessities.

All of these things cost money, and you received them all—at no charge! Be grateful for every single instance, because when you can feel sincere gratitude for the money you've received in the past, your money will increase in the future! It is guaranteed by universal law. So be *truly* grateful for the abundance of money you've been given throughout your life. The more sincere you are, and the more you feel it, the faster you will see a dramatic change to the circumstances of your money in the present.

Gratitude for the Present

The second way to use the power of gratitude to attract more money into your life is to be grateful for the money you have right now, regardless of how much or how little.

When you're grateful for the things you have, no matter how small they may be, you will receive more of those things. If you're grateful for the money you have, however little, you will receive more money. If you're grateful for the job that you have, even if it's not your dream job, you will receive better opportunities in your work. Gratitude is the great multiplier of life!

On the other hand, when you're not grateful, you cannot receive more in return. When you're not grateful for the money you have, you stop the flow of more money. If you are not grateful for your home, however humble, you rob yourself of the chance to live in a better home. If you are not grateful for your job, career, or business, then you will miss out on every pay raise, promotion, and opportunity for increasing profits.

To *receive* more you must be grateful for what you have. It's the law.

Gratitude for the Future

The third and final way to use the power of gratitude to attract more money into your life is to be grateful for the money you want as though you have already received it.

When you ask the Universe for something—whether it's money or anything else—you must believe that you already have it, which means that you need to feel gratitude for having it right now. In other words, be grateful *before* you've received.

When you give thanks as though you have already received what you want, you are emitting a powerful signal to the Universe. That signal is saying that you have it already because you are feeling gratitude for it now. Each morning before you get out of bed, make it a habit to feel the feelings of gratitude in advance for the money—and anything else—you want, as though it is done.

One woman used the power of gratitude for the past, present, and future as she wished for a new car to better suit the needs of her growing family. Rather than complain about her unreliable older car, she gave thanks for it and for the time that they had spent together. She wrote in her gratitude journal about how truly grateful she was for that car, and for all the cars she'd had throughout her lifetime. She expressed her deepest appreciation for the freedom and mobility that her cars had provided her.

When her old car finally broke down beyond repair, she simply pictured herself driving a new, seven-seater family car, and she thanked the Universe in advance. It then occurred to her that she hadn't told the Universe how much she was willing to pay for this car. On a whim, she decided to make it zero dollars—she wanted to see if being grateful would result in her receiving a car for free.

The very next day her husband came home from work to say that his boss had offered to buy them a new car of their choice. This was completely unprompted, and even more curious was the fact that the husband didn't even need a car for work. This meant it would be available for the wife all the time. Naturally enough she got to choose, and she went for her seven-seat, fully optioned family wagon. The boss even threw in car insurance, servicing, cleaning, and a fuel card for good measure. It really was a free car in every sense, and this woman had attracted it by being grateful for all the cars she had ever owned, for her current car, and for the car she hoped to receive.

The Unlimited Ways Money Can Come to You

Anytime you practice gratitude for money, or anything else you want, remember there are always unlimited ways that money or riches can come into your life. If you can be grateful each time your riches increase, you will keep the abundance of money flowing to you.

Money can come to you through receiving an unexpected check, an increase in salary, a lottery win, a tax refund, or an unanticipated gift of money from someone. Your money can also increase when somebody else spontaneously picks up the tab for coffee, lunch, or dinner, when you're about to purchase an item and you discover it has been discounted, when there's a money-back offer on a purchase, or when someone gives you a gift of something you needed to buy. The end result of every one of these circumstances is that you have more money! So whenever a situation arises, ask yourself: Does this circumstance mean that I have more money? Because if it does, you need to be very grateful for the money you're receiving through that circumstance!

If you tell a friend you're about to buy an item and the friend offers to lend or give you that very item because they have one they're not using, or if you're planning to travel and you hear about a discounted special that you end up taking, or if your lending institution lowers their interest rate, or a service provider offers you a far better package, your money will increase through the saving of money. Are you getting the idea of the unlimited situations where you can receive money?

Most likely you've experienced some of these situations in the past, and whether you realized it or not at the time, they occurred because you attracted them. But when gratitude is your way of life, you attract these situations all the time! Many people call it good luck, but it's not luck at all; it's universal law.

One woman shared a great example of this, and oddly enough, it happened soon after she lost her job. She had always been the major breadwinner in her family, and she took enjoyment in paying for her sister's birthday celebrations each year. But with her sister's birthday fast approaching, and now without a job and with no money coming in, there was no way she could afford a big party. Nevertheless she asked her sister how she wanted to spend her big day. Her sister was reluctant, but the woman insisted, and so they made plans to spend the night at an upscale club with their family and friends. When the big night rolled around, the woman gave thanks for everyone in attendance, for all she had, and for the abundance coming her way. Halfway through the night, the waitress approached with extra bottles and the news that their entire tab had already been covered. Apparently, an old friend who couldn't attend had seen photos posted on social media and wanted to help them celebrate by taking care of the bill. The woman's gratitude had paid off in the most surprising way.

Any circumstance that results in you having more money or receiving something that cost money is a result of *your* gratitude. You'll feel great joy in knowing that you did it, and when you combine your joy with your gratitude, you have a real magnetic force that will keep attracting more and more abundance.

So from this day forward, make a promise to
yourself that whenever you receive any money,
whether it's your salary for work, a refund or
discount, or something that someone gives you
that costs money, you will be truly grateful for
it. Each of these circumstances means that you
have received money, and each instance gives you
an opportunity to use the power of gratitude to
increase and multiply your money even more by
being grateful for the money you've just received!

It is so important that you are grateful for
everything in your life. If you're not grateful for
what you've received and what you're receiving,
then you don't have the power to change your
circumstances. When you give thanks for what
you've received and what you're continuing to
receive, it multiplies those things. At the same
time, gratitude brings what you desire! Be grateful
for what you want in your life, as though you
have received it, and the law of attraction says
you must receive it.

Can you imagine that something as simple as
being grateful can multiply your money and
completely change your life?

Be grateful! Gratitude costs you nothing, but it is
worth more than all the riches in the world.

Lesson 6

Imagination and Money

Your entire life up to now is what you have imagined it to be. Everything you have, everything you do, and every situation and circumstance of your life is what you previously imagined.

Unfortunately, many people spend more time imagining and thinking about what they *don't want*. They're turning one of the most wonderful tools against themselves. Instead of imagining the best, most people imagine all the things that can go wrong. And as surely as they keep imagining and feeling those things, they happen. Imagine the best and the highest you can in every area of your life, because the best you can imagine is a piece of cake for the law of attraction!

The Powerful Process of Visualization

The reason your imagination is so powerful is because when you create pictures in your mind of something you want, you are generating thoughts and feelings of having it now. We call this powerful process visualization. Visualization is simply powerfully focused thought in pictures, and it causes equally powerful feelings. So when you close your eyes and you visualize having money and imagine doing all the things you want with that money, you are creating a new reality. The reason for this is your subconscious mind and the law of attraction do not know whether you are visualizing something or whether it is real. And so when the money or whatever you are visualizing feels real, you will know that it has penetrated your subconscious mind and you are forming a new belief. The law of attraction receives those thoughts and images in your mind along with that new belief and must manifest it as your life.

When I was making *The Secret* documentary film, I visualized the outcome I wanted multiple times during a single day. Despite huge financial hurdles and a company that was hemorrhaging money, I saw the outcome so clearly in my mind that it felt as though it had already happened. There's no doubt that visualization was one of the most powerful things I did to help make that documentary a huge success.

Visualizing with All of Your Senses

The real art of visualization involves using *all* of your senses to imagine what you want. If you want to travel to Italy, imagine the smell of pasta, taste the olive oil, hear Italian words being spoken to you, touch the stone of the Colosseum, and feel being in Italy!

> *Likewise, if it's a new home you want, you can do as one family did, once they found the house of their dreams. Even though it was listed well outside of their price bracket, and even though their own home was in a bad neighborhood and was considered unsellable, they refused to be discouraged. They pictured where all their*

furniture would go in their new home and how they would decorate each room. They imagined cooking in their new kitchen, and taking in the scent and taste of their meals in the dining room. They visualized sitting on the patio and waving to the neighbors. They used every sense to feel the feelings of living in their new home, to the point where it felt as if they had already moved in. Within weeks, they actually did. Their own home received an offer within two days of listing, and the sellers of their dream home drastically reduced the price as they had grown tired of waiting for a buyer.

Just like this family, you can take anything you desire and imagine yourself being or doing or having it now. Imagine sharing it with the ones you love and imagine their happiness. Imagine every scene and situation you can with what you want, and feel that you have it already. Try spending a couple of minutes each day imagining and feeling having what you want. Do it each day until you feel as though you already have your desire. Feel the feelings of having your desire now. Do it until you know your desire belongs to you, as you know your name belongs to you. With some things you will get to this state after just one or two days. Other things may take you longer. Then simply get on with your life feeling as many good feelings as you can, because the better you feel, the faster you will receive your desire.

Vision Boards

If you want your desire to come more quickly still, I would highly recommend that you surround yourself with pictures of all the things you want. You can do this in the form of a Vision Board. In creating your Vision Board, you can let your imagination go wild as you place on it pictures of all the things you want—cars, homes, holidays, expensive clothes—anything that represents in pictures how you want your life to be.

If you are good with Photoshop, then you can put yourself in the picture—traveling the world, driving a sports car, attending gala events and mixing with famous people. Or you can use your graphic skills to mock up a bank statement showing a million-dollar balance, or create the deed to a new home. I know of one man who created a photo ID card for a company he wished to work for and then stuck that to his Vision Board—and it worked; it helped him secure the job.

Vision Boards work so well because they are a constant visual reminder; every time you look at your Vision Board, you are imprinting the picture of what you desire in your mind. And as you focus on your Vision Board and give it your full attention, it stimulates your senses and evokes a positive feeling within you.

So make sure you put your Vision Board in a place where you see it and look at it every day. Feel the feelings of having those things now. And as you receive, and feel gratitude for receiving, you can remove old pictures and add new ones.

Make Believe

Another powerful thing you can do to attract money fast is to use your imagination to increase your *belief*. To attract money you have to believe that you already have it, but understandably many people find it hard to believe they have money when they're saddled with debt and struggling to pay their bills.

To get yourself to a point of believing you already have the money you want, use your imagination and start make believing! Be like a child, and make believe. As you make believe, you will begin to believe you have received. And then you *will* receive. The reason this works is because the law of attraction does not know if you are make believing or if it is real. It simply responds to your thoughts and feelings. You will notice as you pretend and play games of having wealth that you feel instantly better about money, and as you feel better about it, it will begin to flow into your life.

To begin playing games, you could download the Secret to Money app, where you play games of imagining having wealth. The Secret team developed this app based around games I created for myself to change my own belief in lack of money to a belief in the abundance of money. For example, in one of the games, you receive daily checks of substantial amounts of money. Your challenge is to spend the money in your imagination in order to keep the flow of money coming to you. If you commit to the games and practices I invented for the Secret to Money app, then I believe it will change the way you think about money, and radically change the circumstances of money in your life.

If apps don't appeal to you, then you can download a blank check from the Bank of the Universe free of charge from www.thesecret.tv. The Secret team has created this check to help reinforce your belief that you are receiving more money now. The Bank of the Universe has unlimited funds for you to draw from, so you can fill out the check with your own name and whatever amount you want. Put it in a prominent place and look at it every day so that you actually believe you have that money *right now.* Feel the feelings of having that money now. Imagine spending that money, all the things you will buy and the things you will do. Feel how wonderful that is! Know it is yours, because when you ask, it is. We have received hundreds of stories from people who have brought substantial sums of money to them using the Secret check. We've seen struggling families pay off their credit-card debts in the sum of tens of thousands of dollars thanks to the Secret check; we've seen unemployed people secure well-paying jobs equal to the amount they'd written out on their Secret checks; we've seen countless instances of overseas holidays and new cars and homes bought by people who credited the Secret check; and we've even seen entrepreneurs attract business opportunities that netted them millions of dollars after filling out the Secret check. It's a fun game that really works!

You can also imagine and create your own games where you are pretending that you have what you want already. For example, when you are driving your old car, you can imagine that you are really driving the new car that you want.

One man placed a Porsche crest on the steering wheel of his Nissan four-door sedan. Every morning on his daily commute, he would imagine wrapping his fingers around the wheel of the sports car of his dreams. Soon after, his favorite

Porsche model, in his preferred color with low mileage, became available at a local dealership. He test-drove the car and fell in love with it. He made an offer, but the salesman wouldn't negotiate on price. The man decided to think it over for a few days, but then the car sold while he was procrastinating. He went back to driving his Nissan with the Porsche crest, imagining that it was his dream car, in the right color, with low mileage, and at an affordable price. Amazingly, the car reappeared at another dealership. It was the exact same one that he had test-driven. The buyer had had remorse and had traded it in at a loss. The man was able to buy his dream car at an affordable price, and all thanks to his make-believe Nissan-Porsche.

While you are pretending or make believing you have what you want, be attentive to your feelings. When children make believe, their imagination is so strong they automatically engage their feelings. Watch little children playing—make-believe is second nature to them, and they will become a great inspiration for you. Remember that the law of attraction doesn't know if something is real or imagined!

Regardless of how you choose to make believe, whether through games or apps or other methods, the important point is to fully engage your imagination. Imagine your life the way you want it to be. Imagine everything you want. Take your imagination with you every day, and imagine what it would be like if your job suddenly took off. Imagine how your life would be if you had the money you need to do what you love. Imagine how you would feel if you could do what you want to do. If you want to travel, then imagine and feel yourself traveling, instead of imagining every day that you don't have the money to travel. Because that is most likely what you have been doing up until now.

There are many simple things you can do with your imagination that will be immeasurably powerful in helping you to believe that you are receiving the abundance you have asked for.

Lesson 7

Career and Business

You are meant to have an amazing life! That includes every aspect of your life, from your relationships to your health to your finances. And it also includes your work. Your work is meant to be fulfilling and exciting to you, and you are meant to accomplish all the things you would love to accomplish throughout your professional life.

If you have a full-time job, you probably spend around 250 days of the year at work. Two hundred and fifty days is over two-thirds of the year, so if you're not doing what sets your heart on fire and fills you with passion and excitement, you are wasting a lot of precious days of your life.

Too many of us have separated the idea of excitement and passion from our work, and we don't love what we do every day. But life doesn't have to be like that. The fact that there are people who are living their dream for their work tells you that it's possible for you too.

What Is Your Dream Job?

Can you imagine a job you enjoy so much that it doesn't even feel like work?

Or that you would do it whether you were paid or not?

There's no better feeling in the world than to have found your dream job and be living it. To work for the sheer joy of it, to wake up and be really excited on a Monday, to love what you do so much that the idea of a long vacation seems boring—that is living!

You *should* love your job, whatever it is, and be excited about going to work, and you shouldn't settle for anything less. If you don't feel that way about your current job, or if it's not your dream job, the way to receive your dream job is through the law of attraction.

If you want to attract your dream job, it is important to remember how the law of attraction works. You know that to attract something you must ask for what you want, believe that it is yours, and then feel the way you expect to feel when you receive it. And it's as true for your career as it is for anything. So don't listen to anyone who tries to tell you that you don't have what it takes to secure your dream job. As I've said before, no matter who you are or where you come from, you can have, do, or be anything you choose.

> *A patrolman with the sheriff's office had a dream to be promoted to sergeant and become a supervisor. He applied whenever a position became available, but he was always overlooked for other candidates who had less experience and credentials. He achieved good results on the written test, but it was the in-person interview that brought him undone. He was convinced it was because someone on the interview panel didn't like him. Each time, he went into the process expecting to lose out to someone less capable, and each time he was right.*

> *Then his wife introduced him to the law of attraction and he came to see where he was going wrong. The next time there was a vacancy, he applied, but this time he believed he could*

be chosen. He visualized himself working as a supervisor, and even started referring to himself privately as "Sergeant." He expressed gratitude for his job and everyone he worked with. He met with the other applicants and wished them all well, encouraging them and letting them know that they would all be worthy of the promotion. When he walked into the interview, he was delighted to find that the person who apparently didn't like him was not there. He was more relaxed than ever before, and he impressed the panel with his confidence and humility and his leadership potential.

After the interview, he left smiling, and went home to relax and release all doubts and negativity. Later that day, he received a phone call from the sheriff offering promotion to the rank of sergeant, just as he had always wanted.

Manifesting Your Dream Job

If you want your dream job, then think about everything you want the job to be. Think about the things that are important to you, such as the type of work you want to do, how you want to feel in your job, the type of company you want to work for, the kind of people you want to work with, the hours you want to work, where you want your job to be, and the salary you want to receive. Get very clear about what you want in the job by thinking it through thoroughly and writing all the details down.

Try using all of your senses to visualize and imagine every aspect of the job or career you want until you really feel you are living it.

With practice, you'll find it easy to imagine having your dream job, seeing yourself arriving at work and walking through the door. It's easy to imagine sitting at your desk or in your work space, turning on your computer, and commencing work. It's easy to imagine looking at your paycheck and seeing a particular figure that you've asked for. When you imagine having that dream job now, you feel as though you have it now, and that's the cue for manifestation!

Just like anything else you want to bring into your life, *how* you will receive the job or career opportunity of your dreams is not something you should be concerned about. The Universe will move all people, circumstances, and events to manifest your desire in an orchestration that would be impossible for you to arrange. So forget about how you will receive what you've asked for and instead feel as if you already have it.

To speed up the manifestation, you might like to try acting as if you've already received the job of your dreams. Get creative—there are any number of things you can do with your imagination. For instance, you could create a new letterhead for yourself, or a business card with the details of your dream job—the company name, your position, and where your office is located.

I know of someone who created an offer letter from the company detailing their dream position, the type of work involved, and the salary. They also went to the trouble of writing several congratulatory emails for them to receive for landing such a great job. Then, after they had made it through several rounds of interviews and actually receiving a job offer, the only detail that was inaccurate was the salary—it turned out to be quite a bit more!

Another thing you could do is plan your commute to work, and then set your alarm and adjust your schedule around your new job as though you already have it.

That's what a recent college graduate did after she had applied for countless jobs without success. She had come to realize that she wasn't thinking or acting as if she already had a job. Instead, her thoughts and actions were saying that she was still looking for a job, and so, by the law of attraction, she would always be looking for a job. That's when she decided to live as though she was already employed.

She started by getting up early rather than sleeping in. She set herself a business-hours schedule that she strictly adhered to. She planned out her outfit to wear to work each day, and she established a savings account ready for her paycheck. She improved her typing skills and computer literacy to be job-ready. And she began hanging out with friends at the end of their workday and enjoyed listening to them talk about work. She also started to use a journal, and she wrote all about her imaginary job. She would write about how grateful she was for her work colleagues and her boss, and how much she loved working for the company. She soon came to really believe and feel like she was a part of the workforce.

Within a couple of weeks of her starting to pretend that she had a job, a friend recommended her for an open position that she was perfectly suited to. She applied, and for the first time she felt convinced that she would land the job. And she was right. The most amazing thing is that when she reflected back on her journal, she realized that she had been describing this exact same job and workplace—she had literally imagined herself into the job of her dreams.

If you ever find yourself looking for a job, then follow this woman's example and start doing whatever you will do when you are living the job of your dreams.

Appreciation for Your Current Job

Even if you don't know yet what your dream job is, there's something you can do right now that will accelerate your dream job materializing: give your best to whatever you're currently doing. Even if you know you ultimately want a different job than the one you have, give your full attention to your current job, and give your best to it. By doing this, you will actually become bigger than your current job, and in time, doors will open to lead you to the perfect fit of your dream job!

But you should also know that if you complain about your current job, and continue to focus on all the negative things, you will never bring that dream job to you. You must look for the things to be grateful for in your current job. Each thing you find to be grateful for is helping to bring that better job to you.

316 THE SECRET TO LOVE, HEALTH, AND MONEY

At the same time, if you're grateful for the job that you have, even if it's not your dream job, things will begin to change so that you enjoy your job more. You will find all kinds of opportunities, promotions, more money, brilliant ideas and inspirations, and far greater appreciation for your work. And you will find that the more gratitude you have for your job, the more you will have to be grateful for!

That's because when you are grateful for your job, you automatically give more to your work, and when you give more to your work, you increase the money and success that is returned to you. If you are not grateful for your job, you automatically give less. When you give less, you decrease what comes back to you, your job stagnates, and you could even end up losing your job. As ancient spiritual texts warn us, for those who do not have gratitude, even what they have will be taken from them.

So think about all the things you could be grateful for in your work. To begin with, think about the fact that you actually have a job! Think about people who are unemployed and who would give *anything* to have a job. Think about the people you work with, and the friendships you have with them. Think about the valuable colleagues who make your job easier. Think about the favorite aspects of your job that you love doing and think about how good it feels when you receive your paycheck.

Sadly, most people don't even feel good when they are paid, because they're so worried about how to make the money last. They miss an incredible opportunity to give gratitude for their paycheck so that it multiplies. Whenever any money comes into your hands, no matter how little it is, be grateful! Remember, whatever you're grateful for multiplies.

Working for the Joy of It

If you have held thoughts in the past that the only way money can come to you is through your job, then let that go immediately. Can you appreciate that as you continue to think that, it *must* be your experience? Such thoughts do not serve you.

In truth, money can come to you in unlimited ways; it's in no way limited by your job or your salary. The law of attraction is what moves all the money in the world, and whoever uses the law correctly is a magnet for money.

Once you appreciate this truth, then you will be free to look for work that you love to do rather than taking a job just for the money.

If you're doing a job because you believe it's the only way you can earn money, and you don't love that job, you'll never bring real wealth or the job you love. Remember, you can only attract what you want when you feel good. So if you don't feel good at work, you can never attract the wealth you desire, either through your salary or through other means.

You are meant to work for the joy of it. You're meant to work because it thrills and excites you. You're meant to work because you love it. And when you love what you do, the money will follow!

Sadly, many people are living a life that has been put upon them by well-meaning parents, teachers, society, or even by a friend or partner. They've accepted a job they don't enjoy because they were convinced it was all they deserved, or because it was a safe or respectable choice, or it would look good on their résumé. Perhaps they started out loving their job, but in time the work has become a grind. They've let job security dictate their choices in life.

At the end of the day, doing a job you think you should do instead of doing what you love is leading a false life. As billionaire investor Warren

Buffett once said, "That's a little like saving up sex for your old age!"

If you find yourself in this situation, it almost certainly means your current job is not your dream job. You need to dig deep and ask yourself whether somewhere along the way you put your dreams aside. So ask yourself:

What would you do if you could do *anything*?

What would you do if money wasn't a consideration at all?

And what would you do if success was guaranteed?

When you know the answer to these questions, you will have rediscovered your dreams.

So shut out what everyone else thinks, have the courage to follow your own dreams, and you will be immensely happy. Even if you think you can't move because of the need for security and your obligations, it's never too late—there are always unlimited ways to follow your dreams, and it is much easier than you think.

It's possible that you will experience doubts creeping in as you think about the possible consequences of leaving a secure job in order to follow your dream.

If you ever find yourself in doubt, you can ask the Universe for evidence that you're making the right decision. Remember, you can ask for anything!

Something Better is Coming

So often when things change in our lives, we have such a resistance to the change. This is because we're fearful that big changes will mean things get worse. But it's important to remember that when something big changes in our lives, it means something better is coming. There cannot be a vacuum in the Universe, and so as something moves out, something must come in and replace it. When change comes, relax, have total faith, and know that the change is *all good*. Something more magnificent is coming to you!

I was working as a television producer at a network, and I used to dream of starting my own television production company. But I would never have done it because I had a family to support, my job paid well, and we needed the money to eat and keep a roof over our heads. I clung to the security of my job with all my might, despite many people urging me to start my own company.

Then, I got fired.

I was in shock. How would we eat? How could we pay for our daughters' education? How could we pay the mortgage on our house?

One option I had was to get a job at a different television network. But I couldn't bear the thought of going back to what I had been doing. I realized that since I had been fired I had nothing to lose, and so, on a plastic table and chairs in the back room of our very humble house, I started working on ideas for television shows. I developed an idea and created a pitch for a show, even though I had no idea how to create a pitch. But I believed in the idea, and so, with heart pounding and legs trembling, I presented the idea to executives at one of the networks. The show was commissioned on the spot, and when it aired it was a huge success and became a long-running series.

Through being fired I was given the perfect circumstances to start my own company and live my dream, and I remain so grateful to this day for that television network firing me. Without them, I wouldn't have had the courage to leave my job, and I would have missed living the most exciting and fulfilling journey of my life.

Becoming Your Own Boss

For many people, pursuing their dreams in their professional life may well lead them to want to start their own company, just as it did for me. Simply realizing that no one else is going to make your dreams come true is a big step. Your boss, colleagues, clients or customers, and even your partner, family, and children cannot live your life for you. You are responsible for creating a life that makes you happy and fulfilled. No one else can do that for you.

Until now, you might have thought it impossible for you to run your own company. But you must try to let go of the opinions, beliefs, and conclusions you have about yourself, because they're the very things that have prevented you from achieving your dream. Don't compare yourself with anyone else, because you have potential inside you that no one else on the planet has. Let go of all the limiting thoughts of what you think is possible for you, and open your mind to all possibilities.

A senior executive at a multinational firm was redeployed to head office in a new role and with conditions that he felt were unacceptable. And so after twenty-five years of loyal service, he made the big decision to look elsewhere. His first instinct was to branch out on his own, as he had always dreamed of being an entrepreneur.

He made some early exploratory steps, looking for office space and technical resources, and all the while visualizing his new enterprise in every detail. However, the risk of giving up job security was pretty daunting for someone who had spent so long as a company man.

At around that time an international competitor to his employer appeared on the scene, as they were making plans to launch their brand in his territory. He met with them and was offered the opportunity to head up the new division. He hadn't given up on his dream of running his own company, but this was an offer too good to refuse. He gave notice at his old job and prepared for this fresh start.

That's when he received a big surprise. Due to economic uncertainty and stock market fluctuations, the company suddenly decided against launching their new division.

However, they still wanted to establish a presence in the territory, so they revised their offer. They would provide financial support for him to establish his own company, and they would become his major client. He got to become the entrepreneur that he always wanted to be, but with the financial security he desired.

The Secret Principles of Success

If you have your own company or dream of starting one, there are specific principles of The Secret that you simply *must* apply to your company if you hope to succeed, and to avoid the pitfalls that many new companies suffer.

The first of these is in the area of competition. Most people, when they think of the world of business, they think of a dog-eat-dog battle to survive. But when you think of business in this way, it's coming from a *lack* mentality, as you are assuming that there's a limited supply. You are thinking that there's not enough for everybody, so you have to compete and fight to get things. Someone else has to lose so that you can win. But when you compete, you never win, even if you think you've won. By the law of attraction, as you compete you will attract many people and circumstances to compete against you in every single aspect of your life. But in the end, you will lose. We are all One, and so when you compete, you compete against you. You have to get competition out of your mind, and become a creative mind. Focus only on *your* dreams, *your* vision, and take all competition out of the equation.

The second Secret principle for business is gratitude. If you are a company owner, your company's value will increase or decrease according to your gratitude. The more grateful you are for your company, your customers, and your employees, the more the company will grow and increase. It is when company owners stop being grateful and replace gratitude with worry that their company spirals downward.

The third Secret principle to apply to your company is to develop and maintain a wealth mindset. If you have a company, but it's not doing as well as you want, then it's most likely due to your mindset—the thoughts you are thinking and the way you are feeling. The biggest thing that causes companies to fall down is having bad feelings about the lack of success. Even if the company has been going well, if you react with bad feelings when there's a slight dip, you will create a bigger downturn in your company.

All the inspiration and ideas that will make your company skyrocket to levels you can scarcely imagine are available to you through the infinite creative power of the Universe.

Imagine success, and do whatever you can to lift your spirits and feel good. When you lift your feelings, you will lift your business. In every part of your life, every day, love everything you see, love everything around you, and love the success of other companies as though it were your success. If you feel really good about success, no matter whose success it is, you attract success to you!

The fourth and final Secret principle for business is that you should *never* take money from anyone without giving *the equivalent* in value to the money you are receiving. This is known as the rule of fair exchange, and when you incorporate this rule as a business practice, you are truly living the law of attraction. Failure to abide by this rule is one of the main causes of a lack of success in business. So be sure that you always give fair exchange in *all* of your business transactions—to your suppliers as well as your clients and customers. If you give less value than the value you receive, then you are taking from someone, and you simply can't take from anyone in life or you will be taken from. Instead, you must endeavor to give equal value for what you're receiving. The only way you can be sure of giving equal value is to give *more* value than the money you're receiving. If you give more value than the money you're receiving, your company will take off.

Whether you decide to go into business for yourself or remain a salary earner and pursue the job of your dreams, this lesson holds true: never take from anyone, either in profits or in salary, without giving more in use value than you were given. In so many people's lives, this is the reason for lack of money, unsuccessful job experiences, and failed companies. So always give more value than the money you are receiving—in your job, in your company, and in every part of your life.

LESSON 8

SHARING AND GIVING

Prosperity is your birthright, and you hold the key to more abundance than you can possibly imagine. You deserve every good thing you want, and the Universe will give you every good thing you want, but you have to summon it into your life. Now you know The Secret, and perhaps for the first time in your life you will be able to buy things you've always wanted to buy, travel to places you've always wanted to go, and do things you've always wanted to do. Along with that, you have the incredible opportunity to be able to *share* your success with family and friends so that their lives can improve too.

You can be, do, or have anything you want, but much of what you want to be, do, or have comes from the desire to share it with those closest to you. If you think about it, without someone to share it with, you would have very little desire to be, do, or have anything. There would be no motivation to propel you to get up in the morning, to work, to learn, to earn more money, to build a company, or create a better life.

It's your contact and experiences with other people that give your life purpose and the ambition to succeed. Not only that, but the joy of sharing with those close to you feels so good that it helps to power even more success.

My Story

In my own life, I was inspired to create The Secret in order to share this knowledge with the world, as well as my friends and family.

I was born into quite humble beginnings. My parents worked hard all their lives, but they never had much money. When my father died, my mother was not only left without the love of her life, she was also left with little money, and she had no income. My father died before the success of The Secret, so he never got to see that dream materialize. But my mother did. She had spent her whole life barely making ends meet, and then after The Secret, all of that changed.

I remember one particular day when my mother called me in tears. She had gone into a store and purchased several items of clothing for herself. She was in tears because for the first time in her life she had purchased clothes without having to ask how much they cost.

If you've been lucky enough to have a parent who has dedicated their life to your growth and well-being, then you will understand how I felt that day. Nothing I could ever give to my mother would equal what she had given to me in my life.

Giving Back

When you've mastered The Secret and you have attracted a life of abundance, you can't stop yourself from giving back and making a difference in the lives of others. The compassion you feel for people is so great that no matter what you do, no matter how much you give, you just want to do more.

When you give back in whatever way you can, no matter how big or small, the happiness you feel in knowing you have helped another human being will never leave you. The joy and happiness you feel is so great that it can make you question the entire purpose of your life. In fact, the purpose of your life is joy, and so what do you think is the greatest joy in life? Giving!

If a person had told me some years ago that the greatest joy in life is giving, I would not have believed them. I would have said, "That's fine for you to say but I'm struggling to survive and barely making ends meet, so I have nothing to give."

At that point in my life, I had reached an all-time low with money—I had several credit cards that were maxed out, my apartment was mortgaged to the hilt, and my company was in debt for millions of dollars. But having recently discovered the law of attraction, I realized that I had to feel good about money to bring it to me. That wasn't so easy, because every single day I was confronted by the mounting debt, with staff wages overdue and outstanding invoices to be paid. So I took drastic action.

I walked to the nearest ATM and withdrew several hundred dollars from my only credit-card account

that wasn't already overdrawn. I needed that
money so badly to pay bills and buy food, but I
took the money in my hand, walked down a busy
street, and I gave the money away to people on
the street.

It was the first time in my life I had felt love for
money. But it wasn't the money itself that caused
me to feel love, it was giving the money to people
that made me feel love for money. Afterward, I
had tears of joy about how good it felt to give
money.

On the very next business day, I received an
unexpected payment of $25,000 to buy out my
shares in a friend's company—an investment that
I had forgotten all about. That money was heaven-
sent—it allowed me to keep my company afloat,
and to complete the documentary film of *The
Secret* that we were working on at the time.

I didn't set out to give money away to bring
desperately needed money to me. I gave it away
so I would feel good about money. I wanted to
change a lifetime of feeling bad about money.
If I had given away that money in order to get
money, it would never have worked, because it
would have meant I was motivated by feeling a
lack of money, which is negative, instead of being
motivated by love. But if you give money away,

and you feel love when you give it, most surely it will return to you.

Giving for the Joy of It

You must feel good when you give away money in order for money to return to you. The reason for this is that when you are generous with money and feel good about sharing it, you are emitting a frequency that says, "I have plenty." That frequency is matched by the law of attraction, and you will always have plenty of money. However, your giving should be a giving without expectation of return—a giving for the sheer joy of it.

People far too often misunderstand this important point about giving. They only give with an expectation of return. That's giving with an ulterior motive; it's not giving for the sheer joy of it and it is certainly not giving with love.

On the other hand, giving from a heart that is overflowing with love feels so much better. In fact, it is one of the most joyous things you can do. When you give from a full heart, you emit a signal of "plenty of money," and the law of attraction will grab hold of that signal and flood even more into your life.

However, you cannot trick the law of attraction. Your giving must be sincere and you must feel it in your heart. If your financial situation does not allow you to feel love sincerely in your heart as you give money, then you should probably reconsider giving money. Instead, you can give in many other ways which are equally powerful. Give love and appreciation to people. Give gratitude for what you have. Give a helping hand, give a kind gesture, give a smile, and give the best of yourself to everyone you meet. As you take action through sincere giving, the law of attraction will respond and you will be given to in every area of your life through people, circumstances, and events.

> *A married couple with four children had found the house of their dreams for sale, but unfortunately it was well outside their budget. Nevertheless, the husband visualized his family living in this house with so much feeling and joy that he came to believe it would be theirs.*

> *A couple of weeks later, the husband was getting lunch at a café not far from the location of his dream home. An older lady in front of him was holding up the queue as she was unable to pay because she had left her purse in her car. She excused herself and went out to retrieve her money. The man ordered lunch to go, and then*

*headed out to his own car. In the parking lot, he
noticed the lady standing by her car looking a
little distressed. He approached her to see what
was wrong. It turned out she had locked her keys
along with her purse inside the car. He asked her
if she had a spare key and she said yes, but it was
at home. He offered to drive her there and back
and she accepted gratefully.*

*As he approached her driveway, he realized that
her house was the exact dream home that he and
his wife had wanted to buy. She went inside to
retrieve her spare key, and he spent those few
moments visualizing living there just as he
had done for the previous two weeks. When the
older lady returned, he told her that he loved her
house and that he would buy it if only he could
afford it. She looked at him thoughtfully and
then asked how much he could afford. He was a
little embarrassed but he named his figure. She
considered that in quiet contemplation, then blew
his mind when she said, "Okay, you can have it."*

*They worked out the terms on the spot, and he
received his dream home at a bargain price. And
all as a direct consequence of giving a helping
hand without any expectation of return.*

There are so many opportunities for you to give
and thereby open the door to receiving. Give kind

words. Give a smile. Give appreciation and love. In fact, your love, your joy, your positivity, your excitement, your gratitude, and your passion are the true and everlasting gifts in life. All the riches in the world cannot even come close to the most priceless gift in all of creation—the love inside you. And so as you give with love, the law of attraction must return to you the sheer joy and untold happiness of everything you want and love.

A Summary of

The Secret to Money

Every single thing you do should be for the sheer joy of it, whether that's in regard to your career or business, or any other aspect of your life. The purpose of your life is joy, and nothing should come ahead of that, including money. Sadly, far too many people place money ahead of their joy and all the things they love to do. They make earning money the purpose of their life. They make money their God.

Don't get me wrong, money and all the material things you buy with it are wonderful, and experiencing them is one of the great pleasures of living on Earth. However, through the conditioning of society we can be misled into thinking that the acquisition and accruement of material things is the purpose of our life. If material things were the purpose of our life, they would provide true happiness, fulfillment, and satisfaction, and we'd never need to buy another thing. The happiness we feel when we get those things wouldn't be fleeting, but would be everlasting.

If acquiring material things were our purpose in life, we would be able to take them with us when we leave. You would walk outside to get the paper in the morning and see that old man Joe's house across the street had disappeared because he took it with him. We can't take material things with us because they are not who we are; while they are part of the joy of living on Earth, they are not the purpose of our life.

Certainly, we all need food, shelter, and clothing, as well as things that we enjoy having because they enrich our life, but the pursuit of material things for their sake alone robs us of the freedom to live a truly fulfilling life. Don't let the tail wag the dog by making financial security and the pursuit of material things the purpose of your life. Instead, make happiness the purpose of your life.

The truth is, every single human being on the planet just wants to be happy. Anything that anyone desires is because they think their desire will make them happy. Whether it is health, money, a loving relationship, material things, accomplishments, a job, or anything at all—the desire for happiness is the bottom line of all of them. Ironically, when you are happy, then you attract all people, circumstances, and events that bring more happiness to you. The happy things are the icing on the cake, but the cake is happiness.

If you are still unsure on how to go about choosing happiness, then simply do the things that you love and that bring you joy. If you don't know what brings you joy, ask the question, "What is my joy?" And as you find it and commit yourself to it, to joy, the law of attraction will pour an avalanche of joyful things, people, circumstances, events, and opportunities into your life, all because you are radiating joy.

The irony is that when you choose joy and happiness over financial security, you will have it all, material riches and a rich, happy, and joyful life.

May the joy be with you!

Rhonda Byrne